You and Your Money

A Survival Guide to the Controlled Economy

YOU AND YOUR MONEY

*A Survival Guide
to the Controlled Economy*

by

ELIOT JANEWAY

DAVID McKAY COMPANY, INC.
NEW YORK

You and Your Money

A Survival Guide to the
Controlled Economy

Copyright © 1972 by Eliot Janeway

Grateful acknowledgment is made to the Chicago Tribune Company and the Chicago Tribune–New York News Syndicate, Inc., for permission to reprint the newspaper columns included herein.

Library of Congress Catalog Card Number: 78-188269
Manufactured in the United States of America

On the principle that the best investment approach works out as good "grandchildren investments," this book is dedicated with hope and confidence to my grandchildren—Samuel Struthers Janeway, age four, and Mary Warwick (Miss Daisy) Janeway, age two.

FOREWORD

$
$
$
$
$
$
$
$
$

I am happy to have the opportunity to introduce this timely and incisive compilation of Eliot Janeway's views on today's critical financial issues. These issues—all the way from federal fiscal policy right down to the burdens and benefits of home ownership—are crucial to the well-being of every American family.

Sound advice on what to do with the money that you still control is at a premium today. For our federal government—which now controls so much of the money that started out as yours—knows far too little about what it should do with it. Prudent financial management had better begin at home; for it does not now begin in Washington.

What happens in Washington establishes the framework within which families find themselves coping with their money problems and planning for their financial opportunities. What has been happening in Washington reflects the double problem that confronts both the President and the Congress—and that will confront the next President and the next Congress.

The double problem is for creative and responsible political leadership to achieve two fair and sustainable accommodations, two "fits" between interests which have all too often been in conflict. The first "fit" needed is that between the legitimate needs of the taxpayer and the legitimate claims of the tax collector. The second "fit" needed is between America's own legitimate economic interests and the interests of our friendly competitors—who are also our creditors—in Europe and Japan.

Attempts by our leaders to evade the claims of legitimate but diverse interests have ceased to be tolerable. Indeed, today we are living with and suffering from the distrust caused by misguided attempts at evasion in the past. At home, the needs of the taxpayer and the claims of the tax collector can be reconciled—but only when the purposes and beneficiaries of government expenditures are candidly identified and convincingly justified. Internationally, America's economic needs can be reconciled with those of our friends—but only when our government is candid in stating our needs and convincing in bargaining for them.

Our government's position of leadership in the world is based primarily upon two foundations: the trust it inspires in its own citizens and the trust it can evoke from other free nations. Without these foundations, military strength will not be adequately supplied from our domestic resources nor will it be respected internationally.

The security our government provides for us and our friends, that is, depends upon the trust our government earns. Fair dealing is the basis for trust. Fair dealing by our government with its own citizens and its foreign friends is the prerequisite for American leadership. Without such fair dealing, and the trust and support it creates, no negotiations with our economic and/or political competitors can pass muster as the negotiations from strength President Nixon has been seeking.

Only when our government has struck fair and sustainable bargains—both with the citizens who support it at home and with our allies abroad—will our government succeed in bargaining effectively with the Communist powers, too.

These great issues of government policy and responsibility have a direct and immediate impact upon the close-to-home money problems of Americans. Domestically, what taxpayers can afford to give up to the government depends in part upon what government provides for them. It is time to balance John Kennedy's stern reminder—"Ask not what your country can do for you; ask what you can do for your country"—with the sober reminder that the precondition for doing more for yourself, and therefore for your government, is for your government to do more against inflation than it has yet done. A federal budget "balanced" in the narrow sense of dollars-in and dollars-out is not enough. We require a federal budget "balanced" between needs that only the government can meet and needs that only private citizens can meet. A budget so "balanced" will be a bulwark of stability and confidence—not the byword for mismanaged wastefulness that the federal budget has become.

In our international economic dealings, "balance" is also the watchword. "Balance" is needed between the relatively small benefits that imports bring to many consumers and the heavy toll they impose on working people, businesses, and entire communities. Subsidized imports that destroy American jobs and drive American corporations out of the country or out of business are no bargain. Only trade that is fairly balanced will remain free. It is all very well to speak of our having evolved from an economy of production into a society of services, but I agree with the thesis that Eliot Janeway asserts in this book. America will not discharge its responsibility to itself—much less to the world which looks to it for leadership for new initiatives and continuing security—unless and until it demonstrates once again the ability of its basic workshop industries to hold their own in their own backyards. Respect for America's national undertakings with other nations hinges upon the performance of the American economy in its competitive dealings with other economies.

How much money Americans will have in their pocketbooks depends upon our government's success in striking the "balanced bargains" I have outlined. The prudent search for balance does not stop in Washington and it will not stop in this or any future year. As a nation, our task in the years ahead will not be to envision yet further "new frontiers." Rather, our task will be to pay for the trip to those frontiers that we deem to be worth reaching. As individuals, too, we all face this task: to balance our needs against our resources and to budget how best to meet our needs. In accomplishing this task, we can all benefit from the kind of insight and experience that Eliot Janeway offers in this book.

Congressman Wilbur D. Mills
Chairman, House Ways and Means Committee

CONTENTS

$
$
$
$
$
$
$
$
$

INTRODUCTION
$
$
$
$
$
$
$
$
$
$

Permanent crisis is a contradiction in terms. Unintelligible and uncomfortable though this way of life is, a failure of leadership has made it inescapable. How are we to adjust our way of life in the present, and our ability to plan for the future, to this disconcerting prospect? Learning how to do so is the responsibility of all of us in America today.

Finding a workable mix between economics and politics is the answer. If the penalty imposed by the economics of crisis is a retreat to the politics of crisis, the hope offered by the politics of crisis is an advance to the economics of normalcy. The penalty and the hope were jumbled into unintelligibility by the crisis of confidence and the failure of performance which proclaimed the economics of crisis and precipitated the politics of crisis in the pre-election year of 1971.

"The government will manage the economy," is the first of the simplistic slogans which dominates the politics of crisis, especially in Presidential election years. "The President will manage the government," is the second. And so every Leap Year holds a promise of a great leap forward past all records of prior economic performance

—in time to pay a political dividend to the incumbent President as his reward for relieving the voters of their pocketbook anxieties. Nevertheless, successive Presidential exercises in economic management have scarcely lived up to this optimistic promise. Quite the contrary, modern history is checkered with costly election year collisions between the business cycle and the speculative cycle that accentuates its fluctuations.

Three hundred years after Sir William Petty, Keynes's worthy predecessor, published his pioneering treatise on political arithmetic, economics can hardly be regarded as being in its infancy. A regression into second childhood is more like it. The retreat of this noble art of speculation into the abstractions of algebra is the most conspicuous evidence supporting the charge. C. D. N. Worswick's 1971 Presidential Address to the Economic Section of the British Association for the Advancement of Science (published in the *Economic Journal* of March, 1972) provides the most devastating documentation. Worswick described economists as "making a marvellous array of pretend-tools which would perform wonders if ever a set of facts should turn up in the right form."

The classical economists were social reformers. Keynes added the indelible imprint of his unforgettable personality as a social engineer cum political adventurer. Like Churchill, he schemed and complained in the wilderness of opposition until the cataclysm of war gave him his opportunity. But the repositories of the conventional economic wisdom in America today are computer-tending romantics. The notion they have that a political year is bound to be a prosperous one is the intellectual equivalent of a throwback to the days when serious scrutineers of the skies were arguing whether the moon circled the sun or vice versa. Their notion of economics does not connect with the realities of politics. This error of omission has relegated the once lively art of political economy (branding it the dismal science was a case of intellectual McCarthyism) to the musty archives.

I am called a maverick because I try to find a connection between the economic mechanism and the political process. Mumbling prophetic pieties about election year economic booms will not blaze a new trail along which political economists can lead their clients in the economy and in the government. The late, great historian Carl Becker was fascinated—like Henry Adams before him—by the reversal of roles between modern and medieval society. None is more striking or more frustrating than today's pilgrimage of theologians into society at a time when economists have been retreating into theology. The history of the last generation stands as a living monument to the wishfulness in this.

The traumatic crash of 1932 remains the most dramatic reminder that Presidential years do not necessarily work out as banner years. The star witness for this contrary view is Richard Nixon. In 1960 he was the victim of the Eisenhower recession; and in 1968 he resurfaced as the beneficiary of the Johnson inflation.

Although *Six Crises* was the title of the book in which Nixon summarized his pre-Presidential career, his Presidency has institutionalized the continuity of crisis. Since 1969, he has ricocheted from one remedial gambit to another with unsettling frequency. But his solutions have proved more cosmetic than curative.

Consequently, the arrival of the 1972 Presidential year

found the American economy in need of the quadrennial Leap Year miracle that had been touted in Wall Street. Yet the great leap forward has not materialized; nor will it. If political management can't produce a boom in the Presidential year which is Nixon's reelection year, how likely is it to do so in a post-election year—particularly in one threatening to be as troublesome as 1973? Time is running too fast against America for her to dare wait for a lucky answer to this question.

The politics of 1972 began by trying to revive complacent trust in the administration's management of the economy. But even while it did, it rekindled uneasy memories of election year sprees followed by post-election economic hangovers. Even complacent opinion-makers began to credit the assumption that the first year of a second Presidential term is likely to prove as costly for political customers as the election year triumph is buoyant for political merchants.

Their sophisticated brethren took to heart the warning by Dr. Henry Kaufman of Salomon Brothers, the scholarly and pragmatic dean of Wall Street's financial analysts: "The review of actual market trends since 1948 shows that, whatever the intentions of various administrations, bond and stock prices advanced from the second to the fourth quarter only about as often in Presidential election years as in other years."

For the economy, the three best Presidential years of the entire era spanned by the 1932 and 1972 elections were 1936, 1956, and 1964. The first post-election year after each of these outstanding years was an unmitigated disaster.

True, pay-as-you-go opportunism in the marketplace

counts a bad post-election year as a fair trade for a good election year preceding it. But the failure of policy in 1972, and the collapse of confidence it provoked, puts the American economy on trial once more. If 1973 is a year in which unfulfilled promises come home to roost, how will the obligations falling due be met?

Another anticlimactic post-election year in 1973, following a climactic 1972, would leave America mired in crisis and battered by pressures too vicious to be withstood without recourse to uncomfortable new emergency crackdowns. A bad post-Presidential year in the wake of a disappointing Presidential year will accelerate chronic crisis into acute catastrophe—exposing not merely America, but the entire world, to the consequences of Washington's continuing failure to conceive politics that are workable and, then, to make them work.

This June, panic struck the sterling market in London. The floating of the pound and the freezing of money movements throughout Europe formalized the collapse of the Smithsonian agreement on international currency values of December 1971. Where previous sterling crises have been localized, this one was not. Its spread threatened to precipitate a crisis of survival for the structure of internationalized finance as we have known it in our time. Beyond the reach of the instruments of finance, a triple political danger has emerged: first, governments have lost their ability to deal with one another; second, they have also lost their power to deal with their own problems; and third, their defense against this double ineffectiveness has been to retreat into nationalist restrictions guaranteed to be all too effective for the entire network of countries caught up in this regressive abandonment of the fundamental international economic freedom that was won with World War II.

Today's revolution in relationships between the custodians of political power and the advocates of economic initiative recalls the revolution of two hundred years ago in the primitive economic society of France. It was anticipated by the new concept of the Social Contract between the rulers and the ruled. The revolution in the making in America's complicated contemporary economic society calls for the static theory of the Social Contract to be supplemented by the dynamic workings of a new economic contract.

The Social Contract was conjured up as a myth aimed at correcting the institutionalized injuries of the eighteenth century. The economic contract in mid-twentieth-century America was no myth. It was solemnized into a formal statutory undertaking to correct the institutionalized incompetence responsible for wasting the promise of the twentieth century. The original version of the economic contract in America called for the government to provide the managerial wisdom needed to insure full utilization of America's resources. A generation of experimentation has brought a confrontation with fiscal bankruptcies.

Not for the first time in modern history, an official theory has collided with a revolutionary pressure turning it on its head. Marx boasted that he had done exactly this to Hegel's theory when he proclaimed the Communist manifesto. America's hope of working its way forward out of bankruptcy rests upon its ability to perform a similar operation upon the economic contract in its original form. For government in America has exhausted its capacity to lead. The long overdue implementation of the economic contract will see the participants in the economy provide the productive new leads needed to guide the managerial decisions of their political leaders in Washington.

The pioneering experiments which President John F. Kennedy launched in response to the prods of Chairman Wilbur Mills of the House Ways and Means Committee envisioned a transfer from government spending to private investment as the main vehicle of economic growth. The constructive phase of President Lyndon Johnson's administration, which was its first phase preceding the escalation of Vietnam, demonstrated the workability of this switch of emphasis. But the Vietnam inflation aborted the experiment; and President Nixon's commitment to continuity with President Johnson's second phase of failure has precipitated the fiscal bankruptcy which only a return to the original Mills-Kennedy approach can cure.

The enormous accumulation of money by the private sector is giving a meaningful lead in this direction. It is filling the savings reservoir with the prodigious new drafts of capital which America will need to do the job awaiting her. Putting this reservoir to work awaits a practical partnership between the economics of activism and the politics of performance.

*Y*OU AND *Y*OUR MONEY

A Survival Guide to the Controlled Economy

$
$
$
$
$ **GAMBLES IN**
$ **GAMESMANSHIP**
$
$

What Shall I Do With My Money? was published in November 1970, while the argument over crisis versus confidence was still on. The purpose of that handbook was to alert money-users to the inroads which the pressures of crisis were making against the claims of confidence, and to show them how to anticipate the onset of the coming crisis. President Nixon confirmed its arrival just nine months later in his Proclamation of August 15, announcing his New Emergency Program.

The emergency controls he ordered reversed not only his well-known "hands-off" policy toward the economy; they also shifted the terms of the continuing argument over crisis versus confidence. Before August 15, confidence had meant confidence in the economy and its markets to muddle along without a helping hand from government managers—if uncomfortably below ambitious financial targets, nevertheless comfortably above the political peril point. After August 15, confidence came to mean confidence that Washington would be successful in managing the crisis it had failed to avoid.

1971's admitted crisis of confidence called for a new politics of crisis; and Nixon supplied it. Once he did, the old rules of economics and the old economic rule books were scrapped. The traditional wisdom of the discredited economic texts had taught generations of students to defend themselves against inflation by running away from cash, not into it. But with the crisis official—and, clearly, it is not going away—having cash has become at least as effective a defense against inflation as it once was against deflation. Using it to buy bargains is again practical, profitable, and prudent.

The purpose of this book is to cover the transition from the pre-crisis period to the crisis period—specifically, to extend and broaden the investment insurance policy provided in *What Shall I Do With My Money?* Before the August 15 alarm, no new commitments not insured against crisis were worth taking. The coming of the crisis has signaled the return of opportunity for money-users. But it has put a new premium on selectivity alongside the continuing premium on cash.

The most useful rule of the road for money-users eying crisis-time opportunities is summed up in the description of how porcupines make love—"carefully." During the pre-crisis period, this meant—as it will for the duration of the crisis—giving an overriding priority to cash and putting the burden of proof on arguments for using any of it.

Of course, everyone who took this advice and played it safe during the pre-crisis period ran the risk of missing the boat if the alarm proved to be false. Admittedly, risks had been on the rise ever since 1966 when the stock market had topped out at 1,000. All of its rallies since have peaked at successively lower highs, increasing risks more than rewards as they did. Even as recently as 1970, however, rewards still seemed reachable enough to make the game worth the candle.

The erratic, wide-swinging market rallies of recent years consistently tempted professional market players to chase stock prices on the way up, and to dump them on the way down. The rallies that repeatedly turned into bear traps rocketed up as speculation on President Nixon's promise to manage the economy—only to fall apart with the realization that manipulating the stock market has been more easily managed for Washington than coming to grips with problems and learning to solve them. Professional market players have wound up shorter of cash and needing it more than anyone else. Their round trips on rallies and reversals have cost them money, not made it.

Looking back, America has had a pretty good run for its money since the last depression. It has enjoyed a generation of unprecedented prosperity under the leadership of Presidents, from Roosevelt on, whose competence at counting was limited to counting votes by the millions, and not money by the billions. It has been a case of economic ignorance being political bliss and paying off for everyone from the White House down. After all, the last time America enjoyed the leadership of a President admitting to expertise in economics was during the administration of Herbert Hoover. Everybody remembers what happened then.

The danger of disintegration striking again began to develop sometime between President Johnson's acknowledgment of the emergency he created in Vietnam and President Nixon's acknowledgment of the emergency he allowed to develop inside America. Of the two emergencies, the one over which Johnson presided revealed greater trickiness at the Presidential level, and the one over which Nixon presided revealed greater naïveté.

Johnson knew that he was overcommitting the country and underbudgeting the government—with the blessing of his economists whom he did not let in on his secret, and who praised him for learning how to be responsive to them without suspecting that he had learned how to handle them. After Johnson had thrown the members of the academic economic fraternity off the scent of the inflationary crisis in Vietnam, they returned the compliment by throwing Nixon off the scent of the deflationary crisis they were provoking inside the private sector of the American economy.

Nixon, like every President since Hoover, cultivated his image as a virtuoso at the elusive art of dealing with people. He departed from tradition in two ways—first, by staking out foreign affairs as his special province; and, then, by delegating the management of domestic politics to his political managers. But he observed the traditional practice of delegating the management of economic affairs to his economic managers. In doing so, he illustrated the time-honored rule of business that the most self-destructive speculators are the ones who do not know that they are speculating. More literally and trustingly than any of his predecessors, Nixon really did listen to the economists—and to those of both parties at that! The more stubbornly factional and divisive his approach to political operations remained, the more committed to the bipartisan consensus his approach to economic policymaking became.

It was not surprising that Nixon found it convenient to listen to his economic managers so long as their reassurances coincided with his political upticks. But it was surprising that Nixon's political managers accepted the same bromidic diet after his political downticks had become unmistakable and uncomfortably apparent. The clients of economists—in politics and in business—have long since been on notice that, whenever economists indulge themselves by substituting imperatives for descriptions, they forfeit their claim to be taken seriously as analysts of things as they are.

The analysis of things as they are has become the overriding priority of our time. Thinking in terms of "must" is a distraction: thinking in terms of "should" is an indulgence. Only by coming to grips with the way things work can governments, and the private persons who in the end lead their leaders, figure out ways and means of making them work better. Survival for political management nowadays depends on the pragmatism of economic advisers. Reciprocally, the pragmatic test for economic advisers is their sense of whether their political clients are guided by an instinct for survival or are hellbent on self-destruction. The latter invariably applies when economic advisers are downgraded from auditors of policy to spokesmen for policy. And private persons do well to run scared when their government leaders do not know better than to be self-destructive.

Men in power are rarely undone by what they themselves do. The fatal flaw generally shows up as a reflection of what they think. In Nixon's case, it took the form of his underestimation of the economic factor in political management. His purely political approach to power politics no doubt accounted for his affinity to Dr. Henry Kissinger, whose airy dismissal of everything to do with economics and finance reflected Nixon's own attitude. After the ill-fated Smithsonian conference to negotiate the devaluation of the dollar in December 1971, Kissinger bragged that listening to the pontifications of the practitioners of financial abracadabra had satisfied him that they made even less sense than he had supposed. In all fairness, he had a point.

Kissinger played his role as "Deputy President of the U.S. for Foreign and Security Affairs" with a swagger that invited comparison with Metternich, and I found myself referring to him as "the young Metternich." I gather that he agreed. But in thinking of him as a throwback to Napoleon's wily rival, it is well to remember that Metternich followed an older imperial tradition in relying on the House of Rothschild. Kissinger saw no need for any contemporary counterpart with financial backup strength.

No such purely political approach to power politics can work today, either in dealing across national frontiers with presumed allies among the dollar-holding powers or with identifiable enemies in the communist world. After all, Marxism did not discover the economic interpretation of history; the classical economists did, and Marx boasted about borrowing the idea from them. Nixon failed to see the application to the economy of Clemenceau's old warning that war is too important to be left to the generals. He assumed that the economy is unimportant enough to be left to the economists. Their blunders taught him better.

It was not news when Nixon revealed his amateurishness about economics. Nor was it news when Kissinger dismissed everything to do with economics with an indifference born of contempt. But the revelation of Nixon playing politics like a rank amateur came as a shock. Rowland Evans and Robert Novak, the well-known Washington columnists, developed and documented this thesis in their book *Nixon in the White House—The Frustration of Power*. When Nixon ran for governor of California in 1962, the devastatingly effective Democratic public relations operation gave nationwide circulation to a picture postcard showing Nixon standing alongside a used car, with a caption asking: "Would you trust this man to sell you a used car?" The irony of the fate which Nixon subsequently invited is that he bought a used budget from Johnson. When he committed himself to fiscal continuity on taking office in January 1969, he invited economic failure and financial crisis.

Nixon's most objective, independent, and competent economic adviser, Alan Greenspan, has stated that all of Nixon's subsequent troubles followed from his taking Johnson's holdover budget at face value. Any President who accepts a fraudulent budget handed down to him by a predecessor known to be a pastmaster at fiscal fuddling would be suspect as a rank amateur. The double jeopardy Nixon invited by going along with economic recommendations based on that fiscal heritage and, then, by going along with his advisers' economic recommendations confirms the Evans and Novak thesis.

No one could fault the diplomatic strategy Nixon relied on Kissinger to devise for him as conventional—his trip to Peking may not have been necessary, but it did win him a "first" for being imaginative. By contrast, the economic

You and Your Money

strategy Nixon trusted his resident soothsayers to package for him was as dull as the stereotyped dishwater served up in the textbooks.

Voltaire created an immortal character as the prototype of the expert adviser who never manages to anticipate disaster and never fails to welcome it. Dr. Pangloss was his name. "Everything is for the best in the best of all possible worlds," was his predictable pronouncement in response to every disaster. The comfort the establishment econometricians gave Nixon was truly Panglossian. So was its reliable echo from their opposite numbers, the econometricians-in-exile.

The arrival of the Penn Central crisis of May 1970, signaled the abandonment of the old economics of anti-inflation as a self-defeating exercise in futility, deemed sound in principle but admitted to be insupportable in practice. And since a primary principle of election year politics calls for making money easy, the elections of 1970 mothballed Nixon's first economic game plan. Accordingly, Nixon announced himself a Keynesian and proceeded to pour billions of dollars into the economy—directly, by spending cash the Treasury borrowed from the credit markets; and indirectly, through the Federal Reserve Board, by pumping huge supplies of money into the credit markets for the government to borrow.

Nixon's successive efforts at retrieval command respect as successes: each of them defused panic and achieved a recovery back to stagnation. In his first crisis, choking the economy for lack of liquidity had threatened to precipitate a panic. In his second crisis, overstaying with the government's hands-off policy threatened to grind the American economy to a halt. Switching to "doing something," he imposed controls on the economy he had been unable to manage, and kept it going in the twilight zone between slump and recovery.

Meantime, however, the expedient by which he survived his first two domestic crises brought on his third. For these successive exercises in domestic economic activism set in motion the forces that precipitated the international monetary crisis of 1971. Inescapably, the American economy, which Nixon took for granted, had become both the carrier of crisis in the world and the hope of averting it.

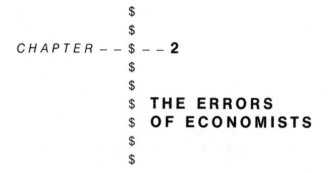

CHAPTER – – $ – – **2**

THE ERRORS
OF ECONOMISTS

Sounding the alarm to 1970's siege of oncoming money trouble was the purpose of *What Shall I Do With My Money?* And debunking the belief that government can help the stock market without helping itself was a related purpose. Its thesis was that conventional economic wisdom was riding for a fall. August 15, 1971, marks the spot where everyone gullible enough to have gone along with the consensus of complacence met their comeuppance—beginning with the President, and including everyone who had believed that things would get better without the President executing a sharp about-face to meet the crisis of confidence.

The failure of Nixon's first game plan—which counted on more unemployment to produce less inflation—was admitted by the adoption of his second—which counted on more inflation to produce more employment. Nixon's second game plan was declared a failure on August 15. Until then, the politicians of both parties had trusted their economic advisers to convert their computers into the economic equivalent of an autopilot system for steering the economy on a predictable course. But after Nixon successively trusted the old economics to fight inflation and the

10

new economics to fight recession—and found them both wanting—his imposition of peacetime controls institutionalized a reversal of role. The President, who had been the respectful and acquiescent client, became the playmaker.

Never was any President cheered with such continuing unanimity by card-carrying members of the union of academic economists. The members of both locals—the Republicans in residence in the White House and the Democrats in exile—agreed right down to the August 15 debacle that inflation was on the way out and that recovery was on the way back. Then, pyramiding their intellectual losses, the members of both locals agreed all through the fiasco of Phase Two that happier (if not quite happy) days were right around the corner.

True, discordant minor notes expressed differences. But they involved minor technicalities. From where the President and his political strategists sat, up or down was the only question that mattered. While Nixon still clung to his pre-August 15 hands-off policy, the economic advisers of his opponents agreed with his own economic advisers that he was safe against the danger of a downturn, even if he continued to do nothing.

After the downturn developed, and after Nixon moved to reverse it, both groups defied the popular presumption which expected them to disagree in principle. They agreed as a practical matter that the recovery that they had anticipated without benefit of a push from the government would be even stronger because of the push the government had given. Confidence that what the government does will work blurred the analysis of the economists as well as the more vulgar speculations of the speculators in Wall Street.

Again, or still, with no sense of contradiction—after months of bipartisan reassurance to a naïve and trusting President that recovery inside America was on the way—the same professional chorus of economic complacence reassured him that America's continued recovery awaited only the promised new underwriting offered by the exercise in dollar devaluation.

The stubbornly optimistic projections developed by even the Democratic economists-in-exile testified that their faith in the effectiveness of government decisions was as impractical as it was trusting. So many economic technicians with political commitments so fiercely competitive could not have been so unanimous in accepting projections so unrealistic unless all of them were guided by a common commanding calculation. They were. Uncritical acceptance of the numbers game, popularly known as guesstimating the GNP, was even more responsible for their critical lapse than their knee-jerk way of taking government decisions as market compulsions.

From the standpoint of analytical self-protection, money-using wisdom begins with learning to recognize the GNP as a statistical and public relations distraction—which is what it has become. During the postwar years, America's complicated economic society has undergone a dual transformation. First, it has been dominated by the growth of big government. Simultaneously, this growth has been affected by the rise of services relative to the production of goods. But since this change in the character of the economy has not been properly factored in, the GNP numbers have been inflated into the analytical equivalent of a distractive soporific. Their built-in self-propelled growth obscures the critical question whether the productive economy is—apart from services—doing more work, or less; and in either case, at what rate. Looking backward, however, in the simpler world of the small prewar economy of 1938–40, the need for the GNP figures was overdue.

Strange though it may seem to those who have come on the analytical scene subsequently, the depression decade had caught the government without macroeconomic data on the overall performance of the economy. Despite the reputation President Hoover had made in his prior service as Secretary of Commerce by his pioneering of governmental statistical services, he had not seen the need for this job to be done. My private collaboration with the famous New Deal "gold-dust twins," Tom Corcoran and Ben Cohen, was instrumental in activating the innovations which led, with the Reorganization Act of 1938, to the creation of a center for economic forecasting and budget control inside the White House (the Budget Bureau has run the government ever since!); as well as for the adoption by the government of the systems of overall accounting subsequently institutionalized in the GNP and National Income Series. By virtue of my participation in these innovations—indispensable in a simpler and smaller world—I feel free to take an independent view of the contemporary usefulness of the macroeconomic data compiled with the GNP figures.

Pragmatically speaking, the analyst relying on the GNP numbers to discern the underlying economic trend, or the financial soundness of the American economy today, is in the position of a bystander at a grade crossing watching a freight train go by. Recording the numbers on the boxcars will not shed any light on either the freight inside any car or the destination of the train. Recording the numbers is an idle exercise in statistical irrelevance. So it is with GNP numbers.

No matter what the trend may be in the economy and its trend-making markets—beginning with the stock market—a built-in uptrend dominates the GNP. Even to dismiss it as providing a count of inflation, rather than of the work done by the economy or the trend of its markets, does not account for its increasing irrelevance to the practicalities of business and investment judgment or of government policy-making. Trusting higher GNP numbers at face value can and often has entrapped the political mind in costly policy miscalculations in governing the body economic.

"All's well" is the signal monotonously flashed with the transmittal of each increase recorded in GNP numbers. But reconciling the figures with the realities—a responsibility that is mundane but inescapable—leaves no doubt that a higher GNP can be dangerous and costly nonsense. For better GNP numbers have recurrently provided no insurance against bad business experience.

The fact is that no recession in sight is likely to be severe enough to cause a decline in GNP. Between the great expansion financed by the onset of the Korean War in 1950 and 1972, the economic establishment has counted no less than four recessions. Every one of them has been big enough to set costly shock waves in motion. But not one of them has been big enough to register a drop in the GNP figure.

GNP purports to measure the dollar value of goods and services—both those produced and those purchased—throughout the economy. *How much* is physically produced and purchased, and *what it costs* to the seller and the buyer, are thus combined in one global number. At this point, the practicalities of analysis collide with the politics of transition. For in that simpler, smaller world in which I participated in the development of the GNP approach, the public sector was not a significant quantitative factor. Qualitatively, moreover, the government still envisioned its function as being essentially to monitor, if also to stimulate, the operations of the "free" market in the private sector. Since then, of course, the expansion of the private sector has been prodigious; but its expansion has been alternately paced and underwritten by the still more prodigious expansion of the public sector.

Consequently, the simple purpose of the GNP calculation has been confused. GNP was conceived as an instrument of the public (or tax-collecting) sector for gauging the performance of the private (or tax-paying) sector. But the gauge it now provides measures the combined activity of the tax-paying economy plus the activities of the tax-collecting economy trusted to compensate for it. No quarter-year countdown on GNP will still tell the tax-collecting economy how to grade the performance of the tax-paying economy, let alone how to compensate for it. Instead, all that the GNP numbers record is the sum of what the two operations are doing separately to supplement one another, or sometimes to offset one another.

The irrepressible increase in public sector operations is the first reason why the GNP cannot fall—short of a paralytic stroke hitting the economy and temporarily shutting down a portion of its public sector. Inflation is another reason: costs have risen consistently, even—indeed especially—during spasms of recession.

The increase in costs is by no means limited to the selling prices of goods on the shelves of stores and on the floors of dealers. GNP's built-in inflationary bias to rise—during bad years and good—is carried by three basic rates: wage rates, tax rates, and interest rates. These rates measure the cost of services—the services provided by workers, by government, and by lenders. The reason all three rates can go on rising continuously, or recurrently, is that each is a source of revenue as well as a component of the cost of living and of doing business. What is paid out to meet rising costs is also available to be spent by those who receive the payout.

As a practical matter, the statisticians do make an effort to separate out changes in costs from changes in volume. Nevertheless, no measure of actual physical volume is possible for the services component of GNP. Yet the expansive thrust of recent years has been concentrated in services. So, increasingly, has been the inflationary cost push. For nearly 45 percent of the total GNP number is accounted for by services—from those provided by policemen to those provided by repairmen. While the attempt to eliminate price increases from the total figures does produce a "real" GNP—which can go down as well as up —the massive General Motors strike in the last quarter of 1970 showed a "real" GNP decline of less than six-tenths of one percent.

The nominal value that GNP places on what is bought and sold could, in theory, fall—as it did during 1930's great depression. At that time the collapse of the private economy drastically reduced tax revenues to government, which cut its spending to match. But any catastrophe that would make today's GNP fall would necessarily be much greater than it was then, because government today is committed to offsetting shortfalls in private employment. Its spending to do so provides an inflationary GNP offset to the deflationary impact of any pullback in activity and unemployment. By the time the GNP numbers added up the damage, the holocaust would already be apparent to the naked eye.

It is revealing, if not necessarily realistic, to visualize a theoretical set of circumstances sufficiently cataclysmic to effect an actual drop in the GNP numbers. In fact, only a combined pullback in government spending, coinciding with a stoppage of inflationary thrust in the private sector, would do it. For example, the catastrophe of another General Motors strike lasting for a full nine months, combined with a curtailment in government spending, would do it. An effective freeze on all wages, prices, rates, fees, taxes—combined with a cutback in government spending —is another purely theoretical alternative. In effect, a reversal of the entire post-depression dependence on governmental initiatives to supplement private efforts would be needed to stunt the growth of GNP.

But no accident of history set the government to work inflating the GNP numbers just when the government started to count them. As a practical matter, the GNP numbers will continue to grow even if the economy shrinks and the efforts of the government to stabilize it fail.

Altogether, the numbers game over the annual built-in rate of increase in GNP no longer measures the ability of the economy's productive apparatus to chalk up rates of gain which are more than nominal. Nor does the GNP measure exposure to actual reversal. Under the worst of circumstances, the trusted measuring rod becomes the analytical equivalent of a tombstone. Under the best of circumstances, it provides nothing more useful than a record of overall inflation, while offering no useful clues to competitive performance for the benefit of policy-makers or money-users.

Perhaps the simplest way of explaining the transformation of the GNP numbers from analytical tool to public relations tool is to describe its method of computation. It treats all dollars spent as equal—whether spent by the welfare authorities on old cans of beans or by IBM on new switching gear and by GM on new machine tools. But, as the saying goes, some dollars are more equal than others in the sense that they do more work, first, at priming the pump and, then, in conserving, channeling and building on the work investment dollars do in their capacity as pump primers.

Ironically, it was Keynes who urged the adoption of the macroeconomic (GNP-compiling) method; and who also pioneered the so-called multiplier impact of the productive work investment dollars do alongside the merely dollar-changing job done by less productive dollars.

Yet as late as during the great 1971 debate over the runaway crisis of "stagflation" in the American economy, dogmatic academic devotees of the GNP as a meaningful method of measuring progress—or lack of it—in the economy were still arguing that any dollar contributed to the money stream by the government could be trusted to do as much work as every dollar contributed by the tax-paying sector of the economy. Far from implementing Keynes's theory, this premise actually reverses it.

Devotees of the GNP method of analysis were claiming

that the economy would be ahead so long as new dollars were contributed to the money stream by government faster than its taxpayers withheld dollars ready for commitment. The disappointing performance of the economy did not shake their faith. But it did sharpen the policy difference between the pragmatists and the dogmatists. The pragmatists held, with Chairman Wilbur Mills of the House Ways and Means Committee, that a dollar's worth of private investment by business would displace more than a dollar's worth of government spending; and that it would do more than a dollar's worth of work—by contrast with every new dollar borrowed for government spending, which could be counted on to do less. The dogmatists maintained that, so long as the government kept the money coming, the source did not matter; nor did the impact.

Altogether, the claims of the GNP counters recall the famous exercises in futility of their medieval predecessors who devoted their labors to counting how many angels could stand on the point of a needle. The submergence of theology by the tides of history lost count of both the angels and the needle. The commitment of the macroeconomic soothsayers to the GNP is inviting a comparable irrelevance.

The January 1972 meeting of the American Economic Association in New Orleans relieved me of the burden of defending my description of today's economists as the modern counterpart of yesterday's theologians. The proceedings provided the economists' echo of a working session of Alcoholics Anonymous. Confession was the order of the day. Penance was offered. But absolution was not forthcoming.

No one is more respectfully fond than I of the vast erudition and creative intellectual talents of Professor Milton Friedman. The terminology of theology, however, intruded on his confession that he had been "chastened" by having "seriously underestimated" the resistance of inflation to his professed cure for it. With characteristic intellectual honesty, he said, "I believe that we economists in recent years have done vast harm—to society at large and to our profession in particular—by claiming more than we can deliver. We have encouraged politicians to make extravagant promises" which "fall short of the economists' promised land."

Dr. Arthur Okun, Johnson's last economic duke, is another intellectually honest and professionally dedicated student. He did not balk, either, at taking his turn in the public confessional; although his allusions were rather more secular than Friedman's. Speaking for the Democratic fiscalists, as contrasted with the Republican monetarists, he admitted, "When we were able to call the policy tune . . . the economy did not dance to it."

But it was left to John Kenneth Galbraith to spice the theological fare served up at this ecumenical session of the reigning members of the economic establishment. He sprinkled pepper and salt on the wounds that were bared with his reminder to all those in attendance: "It is no longer true that St. Peter asks only what you did to increase the Gross National Product."

My own method has been more modest because empirical (if therefore unpopular). In the atmosphere left over from the afterglow of affluence, I have rejected the approach that assumes, consciously or otherwise, that the sum of the parts can enjoy increases while the individual parts suffer decreases. The devotees of the economic consensus have consistently projected continuous recoveries because the GNP has consistently recorded increases. Because it has, they have not been sensitive to the fact that the successive recoveries they have projected have been recoveries from setbacks they had not anticipated. My own work, by contrast, has led me to track the course of the industries responsible for setting the trend; and to infer the likely course of the overall trend from the specific performance of these key leading indicators.

Just as reliance on the GNP has made for optimism with each successive high in the official numbers, so scrutiny of the constituent industrial parts of the American tax-paying economy has left no alternative to pessimism bordering progressively on alarm. Literally, the other side of the coin from the drift to stagnation, and to actual shrinkage in industry after industry, has been the progressive spread of galloping bankruptcy throughout the public, tax-collecting sector of the economy.

Incredible though it may seem to the trusting, literal-minded follower of the daily flow of business news, when a leading corporation in a major industry makes news by forecasting an inspirational 10 percent increase in its sales (and a correspondingly comfortable increase in its earnings), it does not mean in all good faith to be taken as reporting that a canvass of commercial demand from its regular customers has recorded a raising of sales targets. Quite the contrary, the representative corporate management, innocent and conventional, is looking in the direction exactly opposite from the marketplace when it makes its forecasts. It is relying on its "house economists" to feed it into the GNP scheme of things, translating the regular

annual upward projection for the GNP into the corresponding annual rate of participating improvement for
the company in question.

It's little wonder that businesses converting increases in
the GNP into increases in their cash register ring-ups
have been repeatedly jolted into discovering that they
have reckoned without the use their customers have
made of their money—or (what comes to the same thing)
refused to make of their money.

The GNP is no substitute for having customers or making money out of them. Part and parcel of the profit
squeeze has been this pernicious, impractical reliance on
rule-of-thumb derivations of corporate sales to substitute
for the fundamental rule of business: "Know your customer and, above all, know your customer's buying needs
and plans." Suffice it that stockholders—actual and
potential—reacting to management projections of given
rates of gains are unaware that such projections nowadays are generally based on management's game as
pawns on the GNP checkerboard, rather than on money-
good demand from customers.

In fairness to the great tradition of economics, it wants
to be added that this cult of the GNP represents a vulgar-
ization of the emphasis of classical economics on effective
demand originating in the marketplace. Managements
would profit from a lead back toward their proper
responsibility for counting changes in the real world, to
which they are obliged to look for "effective demand" for
their products, by the intervention of the stockholding
public. This would put the burden of disclosure on managements to explain whether their sales forecasts reflect
guesstimates of what the GNP will do for them rather

than what they will do for themselves by doing more for and with their customers. It is appropriate to ask why labor need be on trial to increase its productivity so long as management relies on presumed free rides from increases in the GNP to serve as a plausible substitute for doing better by selling more on a more profitable basis.

Only the contemporary economic equivalent of a throwback to medieval theological mysticism can account for the spectacle of optimism over the overall economic and financial prospect, as measured by the built-in bias of the GNP numbers to rise, when only the total, and none of the component wealth-producing parts, is rising. The 1970–71 recession showed that this can happen. True, individual incomes rose in money terms. But the offset provided by the increase in savings was substantial enough to neutralize the promise of renewed prosperity suggested by the increase in incomes. More serious, the gains in savings measured losses in the confidence needed to generate the will to spend. Yet, through it all, the GNP rose faster than its productive components.

In this period, my own switch to pessimism over the prevailing trend of the American economy puzzled my readers, all the more so because in the past I had provoked such fierce criticism on the grounds of being over-optimistic. But my switch to sounding the alarm had been gradual. My first crisis warning was provoked by the escalation of the war in Vietnam. My concern at that time, however, was limited to the war and to its impact on the stock market and the bond market. It explicitly exempted the then still expansive trend of America's domestic economy, and of the world economy around it.

Indeed, as I explained in *What Shall I Do With My*

Money?—and in *The Economics of Crisis* before it—my continued optimism about the unbroken trend of the economy between 1965 and 1970, inside America and overseas as well, was the first of my two reasons for turning pessimistic about the new trend toward trouble in the bond market and, consequently, in the stock market. My second reason reflected my general view that the stock market and the economy are as likely to move in opposite directions as in the same direction, and my specific expectation that on this occasion they would. In fact, they did.

In *What Shall I Do With My Money?* I was at pains to identify the popular fallacy that the stock market strengthens when and as the pace of business activity rises, and vice versa. Instead, I developed the thesis that, as often as not, the stock market moves contrary to the rise and fall of the economy, strengthening when money conditions ease and weakening when they tighten. It was because I anticipated a strong economy that I calculated that it would siphon enough money away from the stock market to leave it weak.

My switch to pessimism about the stock market came in the autumn of 1965. It was then that the financial consequences of Johnson's systematic escalation by stealth in Vietnam, budgeted by embezzlement, let loose the inflationary pressures which deflated first the bond market and then the stock market. The stock market topped out in February 1966. Since then the stock market as a whole has been neither as free from risks to be incurred nor as generous in rewards to be offered.

Nevertheless, not until five years later did I follow through on my switch to pessimism about the stock market with a corresponding switch to pessimism about the main trend of the American economy. In November 1970, I warned that the mild cyclical recovery in business activity and employment would collapse into a major slump. For it was my judgment that the stagflationary consequences of the catastrophic General Motors strike would soon send the postwar boom stumbling downward in a demoralizing transition from affluence to erraticism or worse. The American economy has not been as high since.

I remained optimistic about the main trend of the world economy for another nine months. It was not until the summer of 1971 that I began to warn that the crisis coming to a head inside America was about to be exported. It since has been. Slump ceased to be a proprietary American product in 1971. It became the number one import of every country with an economy free to import what America had to export.

CHAPTER – – $ – – **3**

FROM COMPLACENCE TO CRISIS:
Before August 15, 1971

Nixon's original game plan had trusted the pinch of unemployment to ease the threat of inflation. But it went further. Singling out the stock market as the Typhoid Mary of the infection, Nixon's advisers had persuaded him that the way to stamp out the infection was by putting down the carrier. They counted on the credit squeeze to break the stock market. But the damage done there was incidental. The target the squeeze hit was prosperity itself. Not only did inflation go unscathed while earning power suffered. The drop in earnings, in fact, strengthened inflation by weakening the Treasury, which collected much less and therefore had to borrow much more.

Warnings of a credit crisis fell on deaf ears—until fire flared up behind the smoke. The Penn Central bankruptcy not only bore witness to its ferocity, it also marked the spot at which Nixon switched game plans.

Squeezing credit out of the system was Nixon's first game plan; pumping it back in was his second. His second game plan recognized that he had not known how well off he was before he let his economic advisers aim their heavy artillery against the stock market and knock the props out from under it. His conversion to "Keynesianism" was re-corded publicly as he pronounced the forbidden fruit of in-flation still sinful but bearable. The advertised purpose of putting the stock market back up again assumed that the economy would follow its lead. Nixon's famous mitt-tip-ping statement, "If I had money, I would buy stocks," cleared all hurdles out of the stock market's way as well.

The launching of Nixon's second game plan—his exer-cise in Keynesianism—was the signal for the stock market to regain its lost vitality. Both the White House and Wall Street greeted the market's recovery as a promise that the economy would follow. Instead, the economy ran into the roadblock represented by the August 31 deadline for the expiring contract between General Motors and the United Automobile Workers. At the time, foresight had warned that any possibility of avoiding the costly conse-quences of a strike depended on government interven-tion. But it was not forthcoming. While the stock market ran up on its merry way from its Penn Central lows of 630 on the Dow Jones Industrial Average to its post-strike highs of 950, the government failed to support its psycho-logical lead.

Hindsight has since shown that no issues in dispute be-tween GM and the UAW were sharp enough to force a strike had the government intervened to set guidelines for a settlement. But Nixon's orientation was political, not eco-nomic or financial. During 1970's off-year election, his bet on the political appeal of the "law-and-order" issue assumed that business conditions would improve. The political strategy that went with his second game plan offered labor a trade-off: a free ride on the labor cost push in return for the free show staged by the "law-and-order" issue. However, business conditions did not improve; labor conditions deteriorated; and the labor cost push accelerated.

Rationalization on the part of the economists had encouraged opportunism on the part of the politicians. But the administration's smug calculation only succeeded in provoking both General Motors and the UAW to join together in a desperate confrontation with the administration. Their joint bipartisan vote of no-confidence in the administration's hands-off labor policy and its strong-arm economic policies produced the great GM strike of 1970. It turned into a more far-reaching catastrophe than even the Penn Central bankruptcy.

The squeeze in which both labor and management were caught was the combined consequence of actions the government had insisted on taking and inaction it had refused to abandon. The classic dispute over basic wage rates and hours was of secondary importance in the negotiations. Instead, two fringe issues claimed primary concern. They were, respectively, the cost-of-living escalator and the funding of retirement entitlements. The UAW's understandable demand that automotive management pick up the tab for these two hedges against inflation, and management's equally understandable reluctance to do so, established the GM strike of 1970 as the first major walkout in labor history to express a clear-cut protest against inflation. Instead of being just another labor strike against alleged corporate profiteering, it stands as a joint labor-management strike against actual government bungling.

The backlash on the economy was immeasurable. Members of unions are not the only participants in the modern economy who go on strike—so is the modern heir of Adam Smith's prototype of economic man, known as the business buyer. When the UAW struck GM, he struck too. The response of business to labor's decision to down its tools was to down its fountain pens. The eloquent measure of the far-reaching consequences of the sympathetic strike in business buying—and, consequently, in consumer spending—quickly became evident in the dismal performance of the other half of the automobile industry.

In normal years, any GM strike spots an obvious competitive advantage to the other manufacturers left free to rush new cars to their dealers. This time, however, the sympathetic strike of business buying and consumer spending hit the unstruck lesser half of the industry as directly as the shutdown hit GM. Car sales by GM's competitors sagged below the unimpressive levels of the autumn of 1969. Their truck sales, even more sensitive to business buying, followed suit. Little wonder that GM decided, after two months of siege, that it had had enough. Mid-1970's mild recovery had been transformed into a major slump.

The GM strike began in mid-September and ended in mid-November. The toll it took of General Motors' liquidity came to a cool $1.4 billion—including just the cash cost of reinventorying, but not the cost of the new contract. The practicalities of the dilemma that cost General Motors so dear made a mockery of the impractical evangelism espoused by Nixon's economic entourage. In encouraging management to take a hard line in dealing with labor, his brain trust had urged their hands-off labor policy as a form of moral rearmament for management.

The GM strike established that the government's hands-off labor policy was an across-the-boards losing bet. Its effect was to make labor more militant while demoralizing management.

Thus, the GM strike—first provoked by the squeeze on family budgets, then prolonged by the squeeze on corporate earnings—literally stopped the engines that run the economy. Slump hardened the prognosis for an economy in which labor had won insurance against the cost-of-living consequences of government's failure to control inflation. Business confidence was down because labor costs were up. Consumer confidence was down because income expectations were down. Income was down because both business and the consumer were running so scared that both were standing still. Commitments for future delivery were down because no one could count the cost of current operations.

More than semantics are involved in the distinction between a recession and a slump. A recession is "self-correcting" because it is due to a temporary overaccumulation of inventories, which depresses activity and employment only until the inventories have been worked off. While they are being worked off, money conditions ease, speeding the remedial correction.

A slump, by contrast, is not self-correcting: it is self-perpetuating. Where time runs in favor of recovery from a recession, it runs against recovery from a slump. The longer a recession lasts—provided it is nothing but a recession—the sooner it can be trusted to turn into a recovery: like a six-day siege of the common cold bringing a return of animal spirits on the seventh day. But the

longer a proper slump lasts, the longer any authentic recovery is likely to be deferred: like a cancerous siege cur-
able only by surgery. No helpful intervention by government is needed to supplement the beneficial workings of
time in transforming a recession into a recovery. But no
relief from a slump is possible without benefit of helpful
intervention by government.

Because the GM strike marked the point at which the
previous cyclical fluctuation between mild recession and
mild recovery gave way to a major slump, its consequences dramatized another fundamental difference between two kinds of money-using trouble—the one economic, the other financial. The losses suffered during
recession, serious though they are, are nevertheless
merely economic. Therefore, they are limited to the last
line of the income statement. But slumps spread financial
distress and, consequently, hit the balance sheet with a
one-two punch—paralyzing its liquidity on the top line
and draining its net worth on the bottom line. Worse still,
they transmit financial weakness from the tax-paying sector of the economy to the tax-collecting sector.

Thus, in a recession the Treasury does not compete
with private sector borrowers; in a slump it does. The
slump after the GM strike was responsible for the seeming paradox of fiscal inflation amidst economic stagnation.
"Stagflation" is the name now given to it.

The "stagflationary" crosscurrents of fiscal inflation and
economic deflation disrupted the finance markets, dried
up the wellsprings of confidence, and held back commit-
ment-making in the private sector. In the process, they
reversed not only the trend of the economy. They also re-

versed the expectations of the economists who had been advising their clients that bigger government borrowings would move the economy forward faster.

As the administration moved to meet the critical situation being created in the economy by the spring 1971 upthrust of the strike cycle, it did not doubt that the old history of the business cycle would repeat itself. But the new history of the strike cycle was already reversing the workings of the business cycle.

Since the Korean War, the alternating currents of recovery and recession in the economy have been activated by inventory buildups and their corrective liquidation. It has been a case of cause, not coincidence. For the trend-making swings from inventory accumulation to inventory liquidation were built into the postwar institution of the three-year labor cycle. The introduction of the three-year labor contract had created the three-year strike cycle, and reproduced the three-year business cycle in its image. When the three-year labor contract became effective, the three-year labor cycle took over from the indeterminate span of the business cycle as the effective controlling stimulant and depressant of business activity.

The way it works is simple enough. Stimulus for business activity is monotonously predictable in the third year of a labor contract. This is when surges of buying to build up inventories anticipate strikes that threaten to cut off supplies. By the same token, the first year of a new labor contract brings a normalizing slowdown of operations into line with actual commercial demand.

A special case inflating the strike cycle distortion comes into play during any period which sees a strike in a major fabricating industry back up into the threat of a strike in major primary industries. 1971 produced such a special case. The auto industry went back to work on overtime under pressure to refill the inventory pipelines emptied during the GM strike. The aluminum, steel and brass industries did so simultaneously under pressure to fill the inventory pipelines in anticipation of the USW's four successive confrontations—with the can industry in February; with the aluminum industry in May; with the steel industry in June; and with the copper industry in July.

Thanks to the stimulus provided by the automobile industry as it worked to catch up with its strike-deferred demands, and to the supporting stimulus provided by the industries that supply it as they worked to get ahead of their strike-threatened supplies, recovery was unavoidable between January and May 1971. But the response of the bipartisan economic establishment to this flurry was to mistake a five-month term insurance policy on recovery for an annuity. Both partners in the optimistic consensus took 1971's misleading strike cycle improvement at face value as a testimonial to the efficacy of the administration's second, anti-recessionary game plan.

The administration was quick to point with pride to the early 1971 pickup in employment and activity. The Democratic economic advisers-in-exile, true to form, joined in the cheerful chorus—notwithstanding their own abundant experiences during their days in office of the boom-and-bust character of recovery in anticipation of steel strikes that do not come off when the economy is not strong enough to support them.

In mid-March I entered an alarmed dissenting opinion, warning that mid-May would see the peak—not only for all of 1971, but for 1972 as well—in business activity, employment, and confidence, as represented by the stock market. I did not pick the mid-May point on the calendar by playing blindman's buff. On the contrary, I spotted it exactly halfway on the calendar between the signing of the UAW's new contract with GM and the expiration of the USW's old contract with the steel industry. In one respect, at least, I erred on the side of optimism: the stock market anticipated the mid-May peak in the economy late in April.

1971's early improvement in every single one of the "strike cycle" industries (steel, aluminum, brass) was soon seen to represent nothing more substantial or self-sustaining than a borrowing from the second half of 1971. In fact, summer's across-the-board, meat-axe layoffs of manpower revealed the spring improvement in the simulated demand for aluminum and steel as the least productive borrowing of 1971. Meanwhile, the industry components of this strike cycle upswing were adding a new dimension to the crisis as they deepened it. The import flood was swamping the industries floundering in the backwash of the strike cycle.

At the outset of 1971, I had characterized it as the "year of Abel"; adding, however, that the USW—led so ably by its president, I. W. Abel—would find the basic industries' employers too weak, and its own members too worried, to strike. The GM strike had shown how labor and management were being thrown together in opposition to what government was failing to do to protect their joint interests against inflation. The "year of Abel" was not very old before the preliminaries to the USW contract negotiations revealed the joint opposition of labor and management to what government was doing to encourage imports.

But the administration refused to heed the warnings of both management and labor against the import flood. Relying on conventional economic theory, it argued that higher levels of imports would beat back inflation by beating down the domestic prices of domestic goods. More than incidentally, this argument also served as a convenient rationale for the administration to buy political and military accommodation from America's trading partners by protecting their penetration of America's markets. As inflation continued its upward spiral, the import flood rampaged and began to tear employment loose from its moorings.

The administration's comfortable calculation represented a throwback to the days when the measure of more inflation was indeed higher prices for factory products, and vice versa. But inflationary pressures continued even though the prices of industrial goods were falling. The pacemaking role in the inflationary spiral was no longer held by the taxpayers in the private sector. It was being played by the tax collectors in the public sector. The miscalculation over imports had overnight turned the chapter of the strike cycle reserved for a spree into a hangover.

Economists ended by spending a full year after the strike cycle recovery of 1971 puzzling over the letdown to which it led between mid-May and mid-August of that year. The puzzlement was largely a by-product of the three-way war of words between the monetarists, the fiscalists, and the administration's press agents. All three sources of the confusion had a professional incentive to claim credit for any upturn in the economy—even one due to the strike cycle whose workings were belying the promises of all three sides of the argument. For a strike cycle recovery works very differently from a business cycle recovery. Need for more motivates a business cycle recovery while fear of less motivates a strike cycle recovery.

The early 1971 upthrust in the strike cycle had started out true to form. But at the very time when the strike cycle called for the upthrust to strengthen, it weakened: the invited speedup in imports had produced gluts just when industry was selling insurance against shortages.

Soon the strike cycle was reversing its own historic pattern as systematically as it had reversed the historic business cycle pattern. An accident precipitated the reversal. The scheduling of the USW contract terminations with the union's various customers invited it. The deadline for the steel mills did not come until the end of August; the end of May was the deadline for the aluminum mills; but the can manufacturers' contract terminated at the end of February. Accordingly, the can manufacturers would set the pattern for the industry as a whole. While the big three can manufacturers were fighting to hold the line, a junior labor negotiator for the most junior of all USW customers stunned his opposite numbers on the union side of the table by offering them even more than they were demanding, much less willing to accept. The moment the union confirmed his rash action, the 1971 strike cycle insuring an inventory-accumulating boom was stopped in its tracks. A marginal manufacturer had set the pattern for big business by giving labor more than it had expected and leaving business with less to do than it had expected.

The administration had been relying on imports to do the anti-inflationary job that only the stabilization of labor costs and the refinancing of government can do. But the import flood was swamping the industries floundering in the backwash of the strike cycle. More serious than the complaint that American goods were no longer competitive in foreign markets was the new realization that American industry was no longer able to hold its own home markets.

The fact that state and local governments were obliged by law to invite foreign bids on their construction and procurement contracts against their own no-longer-competitive home industries brought the problem to a boil. The resultant spectacle of procurement money flowing out of the country, while the flow of state and local government payroll and welfare money stopped, turned the irrational into the intolerable. The months on end of shutdowns in the private sector had narrowed the tax base in the public sector. Local city halls were caught short of revenue and frustrated in their efforts either to collect or to borrow enough to meet current operating needs.

The invasion by German steel of the Gary, Indiana, market for school construction left City Hall in U. S. Steel's home base unable to meet the payroll of its local Board of Education. The subsequent invasion by Japanese steel of the Pittsburgh market for nuclear power plants coincided with the failure by the Commonwealth of Pennsylvania to meet its entire payroll. Even the mighty American automotive economy was being squeezed by the invasion from across both oceans.

In June 1971, Japan's Toyota sales in America were up 67 percent over 1970, and Datsun a staggering 145.5 percent. These gains were not being scored at the expense of European entries in the American market. European cars were either holding their own or doing better, while retail sales of domestic models were no perkier than factory willingness and ability to "buy" them by cutting prices below cost in dealer "white sales."

Compounding this inequity, the efforts of the biggest and best corporations to offset domestic stagnation by riding the wave of foreign expansion had given them every incentive to send dollars out of the country—thus creating new jobs for foreign labor and new sources of tax revenue for foreign governments.

Not that the foreign governments wound up being happy hosts. For as fast as American money exported the dynamic of expansion to them, their economies imported the toxin of inflation with it. Worse still, the American government began to export its budgetary inflation.

During the first two years of Nixon's administration, no less than $10 billion of inflation had been exported to Europe in the form of foreign holdings of Treasury obligations. By early March 1971, the Nixon administration had managed its under-the-rug, deficit-financing operation so well that it had inflated the exported put-away of Treasury paper to about $14 billion.

When 1971's dollar crisis was precipitated, however, it was not this exportable portion of the U. S. Treasury's deficit that the German Central Bank shut the window on. It was the entirely different flow coming at it from the Euromarket.

The origins of the dollar crisis in Europe are rooted

in the definition of Eurodollars. In the accepted definition, Eurodollars are dollars that have been deposited in banks located outside the jurisdiction of the American government. But, since the deposits are dollars, they are also outside the jurisdiction of any other government. As Princeton's eminent professor of international finance, Fritz Machlup, has formulated it, "Eurodollars are stateless money."

As dollars, Eurodollars mushroomed all over the financial landscape, free from the normally strict regulatory surveillance of European authorities. As Euromoney, endowed with its own franchise for self-expansion, the same money enjoyed freedom from the scrutiny and supervision to which domestic dollars remained subject. A phrase from the civil rights controversy in America applies: Eurodollars, compared with domestic dollars, are separate but equal—only more so.

The integrity of any money answering this description is compromised by two deficiencies. The first deprives the currency in question of the governmental backing which any money needs to be good. The second deficiency follows from the first. Because such money is proliferated into the banking system without let or hindrance, regulation or responsibility, the deposits created are backed by no reserves as required by sound banking practice. Stateless money cannot be backed by reserves because only the state—as represented by government authorities—can issue it and only the state can enforce regulations requiring the set-aside of reserves against deposits.

Eurodollars—literally "bastard" money fathered by a dollar economy which assumed no responsibility for its foundlings—added a new dimension to Gresham's law. As fast as cheap money drove out good, the good money poured into cheap money. The very European central banks which cracked down on the dollar themselves per-petrated something like half of the monstrous money-mushrooming exercise. For while nobody wanted to keep America's paper progeny, everyone wanted to profit from passing it around. And what the European central banks had done with the dollar influx was to lend it right back to the Euromarket. As they did, the deposits created by their loans further inflated the supply of Eurodollars.

So blatant was this vast official dollar-kiting operation that, by April, Federal Reserve Chairman Arthur Burns was provoked to attack the opportunism of his opposite numbers. He minced no words in holding the European central banks responsible for the explosive situation set in motion the moment the Euromarket boiled over into the Deutschemark market. He taxed them, first, with inflating the supply of dollars and, then, with whipping up hysteria against the dollar. Indeed, they had been guilty of both irresponsibilities.

Burns would have been on no less solid ground had he also warned the German financial authorities of the reces-sionary consequences for Germany implicit in their insis-tence on revaluing the Deutschemark upward. For the big American import market is the one on which all over-seas, export-dependent economies swing. Their ability to compete with one another—not only around the world, but inside the American market—depends on America's ability to keep dollars moving to markets abroad and to keep goods coming into America.

When the spring downturn in America's 1971 strike cycle contracted the American import market, Japan cut her government-subsidized export prices in order to buy more volume. But German industry enjoyed no comparable support. The panic Germany's financial authorities started against the international dollar cost the dollar its reputation; but it cost German industry and finance its confidence and its dynamism. As fast as Europe's money markets forced the exchange value of the dollar down, Germany's export offerings were priced up. Being priced up into a shrinking market meant being priced out of it. Because the Deutschemark was the strongest of the European currencies, the competitive position of Germany's export industries was quickly seen to be the weakest. Ironically, the German economy came to be the costliest casualty of the Deutschemark's apparent victory over the dollar.

The military aspect of the confrontation between the dollar and the Deutschemark deserves mention here. For the dismaying spectacle of America's "military" boondoggling in maintaining her 300,000 military personnel, with their 200,000 dependents, garrisoned in Europe had added approximately $8–9 billion a year to the dollar glut choking European financial centers. It took the plight of the dollar to remove any doubt that America could no longer afford to subsidize what Europe no longer needed. Nevertheless, the subsidy survived the dollar crisis.

Although the international financial establishment calculated that the weakness of the dollar would coexist with the strength of the American economy, the American economy began to suffer a sharp sinking spell. My own measure of the intensification of crisis pressures had been supported all spring and summer long by my collaboration with Albert Sindlinger. Sindlinger's systematic commercial surveys of American consumer confidence play a significant role in influencing the production scheduling of many of the country's best-run industries and the buying decisions of many of its best merchandisers. Our combined findings and judgments revealed uncanny confirmation of his exercises in qualitative reportage and mine in quantitative reportage. Each of us agreed in sighting depression as the danger, and decisive government initiative as the need.

Throughout the spring of 1971, Sindlinger's surveys had indicated that some 5 million households expected unemployment to be higher six months ahead of the date they were asked. By the end of July, his surveys revealed a runaway in employment fears, forcing a collapse in the already weak confidence of consumers. The number of households fearing unemployment by the turn of the year shot up to 12 million, or no less than approximately 20 percent of the nation's total—a full-fledged depression level.

Subsequent findings signaled the surfacing of mass fear of unemployment into a consumer panic: it was a case of the unemployment fear being father to the savings thought. This phenomenon of mass panic running cash into the banks—instead of out of them, as in past panics —reversed another historical pattern long considered axiomatic. The millions of representative participants in the economy who had the good sense to trust cash in the bank as their best defense against inflation, and its by-product of slump, wrote an influential footnote to the history of economic theory. For the behavior foretold the failure of Professor Milton Friedman's famous monetarist theory which, simply put, treats a buildup of money in the banks as a direct cause of a follow-through buildup in the economy.

Sindlinger's surveys were clearly demonstrating that, this time, the buildup of cash in the banks was the result of a rundown in the economy. Pragmatism emerged the clear victor over dogma in this decisive passage-at-arms between economic facts and economic theories.

The range of Sindlinger's surveys extended to investor confidence as well as to consumer confidence. His soundings of popular intentions to buy stocks confirmed his findings of the slippage west of Wall Street. By summer, a bare 8 percent of the telephone-listed public was voicing any plans to buy stocks—an all-time low for a structure of stock prices eroding for lack of broad-based public participation. For unemployment was hitting first and hardest at the top of the labor force, taking its severest toll among the better-trained, better-paid members of the salariat, who also happened to be the most sensitive to the demoralized stock market.

In America, where over 30 million individuals participate directly in the stock market, major market movements have become both the cause and the effect of major swings in consumer expectations and behavior. Unlike the far narrower and more professional London stock market, Wall Street is causally linked to both the real and anticipated condition of the nation's businesses. While the stock market is quite capable of being up while the economy is down—and again and again is—nevertheless, its performance is always an important barometer of how people with money feel, and not only those with money to put into the stock market.

One of Sindlinger's most arresting correlations suggested a connection between fluctuations of confidence on the part of blue collar workers and the fluctuations in the stock market. His surveys confirmed the long-standing suspicion among market sophisticates that businessmen are as consistently wrong in their guesses about the stock market as yesterday's odd lotters. But they also suggested that any time blue collar nonstockholders feel better about their prospects six months hence, the stock market does better eight weeks later, and vice versa. Reciprocally, the stock market has become a leading indicator of attitudes and decisions among enough of the country's households to be influential in exerting a major influence over consumer spending, saving, borrowing, and investing.

My own alarm over 1971's across-the-board progress from complacence to crisis was in striking contrast to the complacence still chorused by the professional consensus. The econometricians greeted the economic demoralization of mid-1971 with a unanimous projection of onward and upward—but their logic was innocent of the real world beyond the reach of their GNP measuring rods. While they were content with measuring "improvement," I set out to overcome the inertia responsible for the deterioration.

My purpose went beyond the guessing game about what the economy had been doing. It recognized that the economy could not do better until, first, it was saved from doing worse. And it went beyond merely calling on the government to undertake remedial actions. It assumed that nothing would be done, despite the deterioration in the situation, until somebody moved to shake the White House out of its complacence.

My efforts were directed to answering the question of "who" as well as "what." Three men—all chairmen—filled the bill. Two enjoyed independent positions of great power and were free to take the initiative; but the third was subject to the iron discipline of the White House apparatus. Chairman Wilbur Mills, of the House Ways and Means Committee, and Chairman Arthur Burns, of the Federal Reserve Board, were the two powers who could take the initiative. Chairman Paul McCracken, of the Council of Economic Advisers, was the loyal and competent functionary who could provide the confirmation. As I saw the situation, convergent actions by all three were needed to wake Nixon to the sense of the country's jeopardy—and, therefore, his own.

Although I played a role as catalyst between Mills and Burns, I scrupulously refrained from having any direct contact with McCracken—lest the White House's prejudice against any presumed political motives of mine destroy McCracken's already limited usefulness as a dissenter inside the White House. Moreover, direct dealing on my part with him would have been superfluous as well as counterproductive. I knew that McCracken had the benefit of continuous briefings from his longtime friend, Sindlinger, and that he was aware of Sindlinger's more recent collaboration with me. Sindlinger's findings confirmed his misgivings about the danger of a business panic, and aroused a sense of urgency about the risk Nixon was running.

While bearers of ill tidings are notoriously unwelcome in their masters' houses, McCracken carried the message to the deputy president for politics, Charles Colson. In thus alerting Nixon's political troubleshooter, McCracken succeeded in spurring Nixon and his econometric outriders into awareness that disaster was in fact at hand. By tuning Colson in to Sindlinger's switchboard, Paul McCracken did more to save Nixon, and to help Nixon get a second chance to save the situation, than anyone but Nixon's public critics.

Although McCracken's chairmanship imprisoned him inside the White House, Mills's and Burns's were bastions of independence. Nevertheless, so long as they took their stands independently, they could not hope to be effective. But the moment the collaboration between these two formidable figures materialized, their convergent dissents were joined in a pincer play. Its July pinch, combined with McCracken's role as the inside catalyst, forced Nixon to recognize the accelerated panic among consumers. The result was Nixon's August 15 switch.

While Chairman Mills had calculated on giving Nixon time to make his game plan work, Chairman Burns was impatient because Nixon had dissipated so much time talking about inflation and done so little to stop it. In mounting his part of the pincer play, Burns chose a Democratic-chaired Congressional committee as the forum for announcing that "the rules of economics are not working in quite the way they used to." He enlisted his unrivaled professional authority, intellectual integrity, and political independence in the quest to form new rules that would work where the old ones had not.

It was one thing for Chairman Burns to serve notice on the academic economic establishment that new rules of economics were needed. It was another for Chairman Mills to serve the same notice on the world of Democratic Presidential hopefuls, whose economic advisers had

given Nixon his blueprints for his Keynesian game plan.
Mills's move came as a salutary reminder to any and all
Democratic Presidential hopefuls that me-tooing White
House guesstimates of happy GNP numbers would not be
good enough.

Nixon's complacence about the economic crisis in the
making was advertised on July 15 when he announced
his China trip. But it was on that same day that Mc-
Cracken handed Nixon two sheets of paper—one bearing
his resignation and the other Sindlinger's irrefutable tab-
ulated conclusion that standing pat was an invitation to
panic. A day later, on July 16, Mills made the first of two
remarkable speeches. He called for a double switch and
demanded that it be made promptly. Carrying on the tradition of Kennedy's promise and Johnson's performance,
he offered a tax cut in return for a spending cut.

It had been in April—just when the 1971 upswing was
peaking out—that Burns had called for a strong American
response to the German Central Bank's decision to cease
to buy dollars. On July 29, in the second of his two public
ultimata, Mills seconded the motion by calling on Nixon
to extend the scope of the overdue emergency program to
the international arena. He warned the President that no
purely domestic economic and fiscal responses to the
emergency could be expected to work unless supported
by an even more fundamental response aimed at the international roots of the emergency. As I wrote twelve
days before President Nixon's declaration made crisis official: the old slogan, "America first" has suddenly surfaced
as the world's last hope of saving the world from the dis-
astrous consequences of an American depression. What
remained was the challenge of how to put America first.

CHAPTER – – $ – – **4**

$
$
$
$
$
$ **FROM COMPLACENCE**
$ **TO CRISIS:**
$ *After August 15, 1971*
$

Whether the government had got itself and, therefore, everyone else into trouble had been the question until August 15, 1971. The Presidential Proclamation of Emergency resolved the argument. How the Nixon administration proposed to dig itself out, and to lead everyone back to safety, became the question when the country went to work on the morning of August 16.

Every President, in his capacity as political leader, writes his chapter in the history books with his own individual style. Each new President presents a challenge packaged with his policies. The country's response determines his success or failure.

Nixon's way of managing the dramatics of Presidential politics was as distinctive as that of each of his predecessors. Where President Johnson's response to crisis was to sulk and complain that the country had let him down; where President Kennedy made a virtue of adversity; where President Eisenhower projected his personality above the level of mere problems; where President Truman—and here the contrast was most stark—won sympathy by wisecracking that "to err was Truman"; President Nixon never made a mistake. Instead, he merely changed course. This is what he did on August 15.

Nixon enacted his managerial role as the mature embodiment of the young man on the flying trapeze. He swung back and forth from extremes of complacence to extremes of crisis. Consistently, his respites of complacence proved unrealistic. Repeatedly, his sieges of crisis promised to be temporary. As fast as he activated the politics of crisis, he acknowledged the economics of crisis. First, the mid-1970 derailment of the Penn Central turned him into a Keynesian. Then, the 1971 stoppage of the economy turned him into a Rooseveltian. Each of these efforts to move the country forward represented an exercise in turning the clock back. Therefore, both failed.

When Nixon abandoned his economic advisers and surrendered to his political critics, he at least formalized the crisis even if he did not manage to come to grips with it. On the face of it, his switch from "standing pat" to "doing something" laid bare a failure in the economic mechanism of the country and the bankruptcy of its fiscal structure.

Exorbitant though the cost of this double jeopardy had been, it was not critical. The complacence of the professional establishment was. Not only had 1971's smug economics of complacence invited its climactic politics of crisis. Worse still, once the crisis arrived, the establishment reaction had been to deny its threat. Instead, the official chorus—echoed as ever by its loyal opposition—predicted a happier end for 1971, as well as a prosperous beginning for 1972. No end of higher GNP numbers were cited to prove it. True, as fast as the GNP numbers were inflated, targets for the Treasury's share of it were deflated. Nevertheless, assertions of confidence by government were answered by expressions of no confidence on the part of its tax-paying customers. And, in turn, the deflation of Treasury collections from taxpayers was translated into the inflation of government borrowings.

Each successive tilt of the greed-fear ratio toward fear had put the White House on notice to improvise yet another charade to quiet the fears of its audience. But staging spectaculars is a temporary substitute for improvising marketplace workability. Twice Nixon achieved a successful public relations response to emergency only to see each fail to prime the economic pump. With his second failure, government lost its leadership role by default.

The government is not likely to recover its lost knack of tilting the greed-fear ratio back toward prosperity until its marketplace audience has enacted the classic Roman ceremonial of "thumbs up" in the economic arena. As a matter of market practicality, by the time the government has been prodded into discharging its managerial role responsibly, those it helps first will be those who have already helped themselves. In any case, the precondition of solving problems is recognizing them.

It was Dr. Samuel Johnson who observed that "when a man knows he is to be hanged, it concentrates his mind wonderfully." Although he happened to be philosophizing about people in general, he might as well have been particularizing about people who concentrate their minds on hanging onto their money instead of being hung with its loss. People with a stake in their own survival are closer to pocketbook realities than governments with a vested interest in putting prestige above performance.

A simple illustration serves to dramatize the transformation of the government's role from economic policymaker to governing troublemaker—and explains the failure of Nixon's New Economic Program. Visualize a building on fire. A passerby sees it and sounds the alarm. Meanwhile, residents trapped by the flames are hanging out of the windows, screaming for help. A crowd gathers, unable to do anything but stand and stare. Finally, the fire engines arrive, led by the fire chief. The sirens screech, the bells clang and the crowd makes way. Sighs of relief go up as the firefighters charge through—only to join the crowd watching the tragedy.

This frustrating scene illustrates the first phase of America's rendezvous with crisis under Nixon. An even more frustrating sequel illustrates the second. The firemen stand watching as the building crumbles and its victims perish—and then decide to go into action. They rush for their hoses, only to find that some of them won't unwind, those that do have no nozzles, and those with nozzles refuse to pump water.

The fire chief, in this case the President, was able to claim his full share of political credit for "doing something." The subsequent damage suffered by the structure seemed at the time to be incidental to the success of the emergency operation. In other words, the operation was a success, but the patient remained on the critical list.

During 1971's start-up journey of the economy from crisis to complacence, my expressions of alarm had placed me in an intellectual no-man's-land somewhere between irrelevance and hysteria. When 1971's economy was propelled back on its swing from crisis to complacence, I particularized my warning. Irrelevance still flanked it on one side; but unintelligibility now flanked it on the other.

No press assessment of Nixon's August 15 switch could have been more unintelligible than its first reaction to my role. It credited me with (shades of Keynes) a successful "essay in persuasion." (J. M. Keynes's *Essays in Persuasion* was one of his more engaging nontechnical books, which actually succeeded at the time in persuading no one of anything except its author's cleverness.) To credit me as a political catalyst would have been more accurate.

I promptly corrected the London *Sunday Times* when it suggested that I was the secret author of the New Economic Program. And in a widely quoted interview with the Associated Press, I branded Nixon's emergency program as an exercise in plagiarism. For the President's laundry list of cleanup measures had been taken over piecemeal from his critics with hardly an effort to weld it into a coherent and intelligible program.

As I have explained, the crisis Nixon faced in August 1971 stemmed from three interrelated problems. The first was readily measurable in the squeeze on America's tax-paying economy and, therefore, it called for remedial economic policies. The second was rapidly becoming immeasurable in the bankruptcy of America's tax-collecting economy and, therefore, was fiscal in character. The third was then still barely measurable in the ominous switch from expansion to contraction in the surrounding world economy and, therefore, was international in character. The big question was whether Nixon's August 15 response to the crisis would resolve the problems.

As events were quick to demonstrate, it was a far cry from merely "doing something" to doing what was necessary. Consequently, as fast as Nixon won applause for his efforts to do something, he provoked pressure to do something else. His exercises activated a race between the plausible and the workable, with the plausible never making it to the finish line and the workable never getting off the mark.

Before Nixon had allowed the crisis to get ahead of him, purely domestic remedies would have sufficed. By the time he was responsive, his first line of defense had moved overseas. Therefore, an effective international initiative was needed to provide cover for the domestic emergency actions that were then overdue.

A domestic buyers strike—by business and consumers alike—had accounted for the immediate problem posed by the emergency for the administration. Although aware of the need to get the domestic dollar economy moving, Nixon found himself on notice to do something even more drastic to shore up the international dollar economy. His response was to shock the foreign establishment into giving him time.

If the White House strategy was not wise, nevertheless it was shrewd. Domestically, time was needed for the administration, as well as management and labor, to clear the roadblocks in the way of reactivating the economy. Therefore, time was the precious commodity Nixon tried to buy with his international program. And he needed all the time he could buy.

On the international side of the problem, time was for sale—but in return for consideration offered. The foreign dollar-holding powers were anxious to make the sale; the administration was anxious to buy the accommodation; and cost was no consideration.

Nixon's double calculation assumed that buying time would begin by helping him on the foreign dollar front while he took advantage of the respite to help himself on the domestic economic front. His calculation was realistic

—that is, provided that he used the time he bought to build defenses against fiscal disaster on the domestic front. He failed to do so; and the resultant surge in the government's money-raising needs left him doing no better than merely slowing down the foreign movement against the dollar. The foreign dollar-holding powers sped it up again as soon as they satisfied themselves that he had failed to use his borrowed time to bring his budget problem under control.

But Nixon made up for his inability to communicate persuasively either with the mass participants in the domestic economy or with the class in control of dollar holdings abroad. He succeeded in seducing the highly impressionable money managers in control of the stock market. And what had been an unstable stock market when Nixon began to woo it became even more so as the romance progressed.

Nixon's manipulation of Wall Street morale recalled Johnson's tour de force in his dealings with the members of the professional economic forecasting fraternity. Johnson first persuaded them of his responsiveness to their theories and then bent them to serve his purposes. In the same way, the stock market recovered from its traumatic 1969 victimization by Nixon's inflationary game plan in the firm belief that it had learned how to make Nixon responsive to it. Instead, he showed himself a pastmaster at a new public relations routine calculated to handle it.

Because the administration was in the political business of answering emergency alarms, and not in the operational business of coping with their sources, Nixon accommodated himself to this susceptibility of the stock market. For, putting the cart before the horse, the stock market jumped to the conclusion that the international side of the three-way emergency claimed top priority over the economic side and the fiscal side.

Accordingly, quieting fears of an international monetary flare-up was given first priority in Nixon's emergency program. The more serious fear of a failure inside the domestic American economy—more serious, as events were to demonstrate, than even a breakdown of international financial cooperation—was relegated to second place. The biggest danger of all—of a disaster in America's ability to finance her mushrooming budget deficit—was discounted as merely trivial and consigned to third place.

When the backlash in the marketplace was felt, this smug order of priorities was reversed—not casually, but precisely. By then, the damage done to the domestic dollar budget easily claimed top priority over the slippage suffered by the domestic economy and the setbacks scored against the international dollar. Moreover, the damage done to the domestic budget, traditionally counted on to help the domestic economy, turned out instead to hurt it. Weakness in international bargaining is the inescapable consequence for America of desperation in domestic government financing, which in turn reflects disappointment in domestic economic operations. It was little wonder that, when the government turned up broke and the economy did not turn up prospering, the international dollar buckled under pressure.

The irrepressible controversy about gold jumbled the unorthodox specifics with the standard slogans of devaluation. The advertised embargo on gold sales was meaningless. Long before August 15 the Washington authorities had stopped selling gold, except in large quantities on a negotiated basis to friendly central banks. When the dust settled, the question about gold was more up in the air than ever.

The December agreement to mark the pegged price of gold up from $35 to $38 against the devalued dollar was scarcely meaningful in the then $43 gold market. With the subsequent spectacular surge of the gold market—up almost 50 percent in only three months—the renegotiated $38 gold price became positively meaningless.

The arrangement would have inspired more confidence, and unsettled less, if it had either ignored the problem or refrained from this implausible effort at a solution. No sooner was the $38 price agreed on than it raised more questions than it answered. For the dollar-holding powers demanded free convertibility from dollars into gold. But the "tokenist" logic of the nominal price increase assumed that the dollar would remain nonconvertible. All that was settled was the defensive stance of the dollar and the certainty of continued uncertainty.

Of the two international measures adopted, the 10 percent import surcharge was the meaningful one. The gold move was merely offered as a rearguard action against Europe's initiative. The surcharge was aimed at serving notice of a momentous change in America's approach to the international bargaining table. From the outset of the postwar era, America had been intent on helping her clients to become her customers and competitors. Now that they had become her creditors, America was beginning to recognize that it behooved her to help herself.

The surcharge was effective as a political bargaining counter if not as an economic defense mechanism. For it advertised the weakness of the dollar-holding powers as soon as they were confronted with the reality of shrinkage in the American economy and forced to pay a toll for access to it.

Unfortunately, the surcharge missed its market target and blurred into an exercise in political overkill. For, politically, the shock to Europe's confidence was more than Europe was able to bear. Economically, the levy on Japan's business was less than Japan was prepared to recognize as costly. Financially, Europe and Japan were more than strong enough to retaliate. Europe did so by threatening to precipitate a dollar panic to bring the dollar down. Japan, characteristically content with the propaganda of the deed, merely brought her own selling prices down by the expedient of raising her normal government subsidies to her exporters.

It was not the drop in exports to Europe that had been responsible for the failure of America's domestic economy. Therefore, Europe was neither the source of America's domestic economic shrinkage nor the target of the import surcharge. Japan was the effective source of the uneconomic and intolerable assault on the American market. At least American industry enjoyed the satisfaction of participating in Europe's achievements outside America. But American industry was barred from participating in the breakthroughs Japan scored in the American market. Ironically, Japan was the only one of America's competitors to put barriers in the way of her direct overseas investment: Japan reserved its overpriced home market for its own lower-cost producers.

The economic consequences of the surcharge hurt the

world economy; and the damage inflicted was the result of three Japanese countermoves. The first two were economic. The third was financial.

Japan's first countermove to relieve her distress was to confront her own sources of iron ore, coal, bauxite, copper, and other raw materials with demands for "contributions" so hardfisted that they "out-Connallyed" Connally. She forced all her suppliers—from Australia to Canada, and including the United States—to accept depression-scale price cuts as well as cutbacks in tonnage.

Her second countermove cashed in on the cost advantage of these "contributions" forced from her overseas suppliers. She mounted a massive dumping offensive against Europe's markets just when Europeans were discovering that their economies, too, were coming down with the "Anglo-American disease" of stagflation.

Japan's financial riposte was the simplest, and was the direct result of the economic weakness her first two countermoves had uncovered at the core of her former center of economic strength. Japan simply absorbed the surcharge. Her previous export breakthroughs, reinforced by her retaliatory import price-cutting, had given her more than enough in the way of foreign exchange to subsidize this countermove.

Any pricing mechanism works only in free economies; and Japan's technology-intensive export sector is the cartellized economic equivalent of a disciplined military organization. Relying on a price mechanism like an import surcharge to check it is like trying to drive through a London traffic jam on the American side of the road. It was the record made by her steel industry that provided proof—if any was needed—that Japan could sustain her attack on the shrinking American market. During each of the four months, while the surcharge was still in effect— despite the on-again, off-again American dock strike— Japan's steel imports into America rose.

When the surcharge had been adopted, only one calculation was crucial: whether American business buying would be reactivated. A demonstration of the government's determination to get the foreigner off his back was the business buyer's condition to begin buying again. And not until then was there any chance that the consumer would begin spending again. But getting the government to "stand up for America" was the prerequisite for a revival of both business buying and consumer spending. "Wait and see" was the watchword throughout the economy until the government did.

Nixon gave away his option on both domestic and foreign bargaining when he surrendered the surcharge and got nothing in return. Nixon's surrender illustrated for the umpteenth time the disadvantage rooted in America's approach to the dollar-holding powers at the bargaining table. America has subordinated her need to keep abreast of her competitors to her outworn claim to lead them politically and to protect them militarily. But her competitors have consistently and insistently put their needs first (which is scarcely a provocation for criticism, as failure to do so certainly is).

Ironically, America's willingness to continue shouldering the burden of Europe's security has underwritten for all of Europe—and particularly for Germany—the opportunity to enjoy export prosperity because of freedom from arms commitments. But Europe's military security today no longer depends on the presence of America's tourists in uniform (known officially as the Army of Occupation). The deployment of something like 7,500 tactical nuclear weapons has offered Europe a combat-ready deterrent to the unthinkable spectacle of a Russian blitz against the West; while the American nuclear shield based inside America gives Europe her ultimate protection.

Meanwhile, NATO has aged from a bureaucracy into a relic: witness Germany's new Ost Politik commitment to conciliation with the East. Today, NATO's nominal capability confronts Russia only in the Mediterranean theatre —where none of America's major NATO allies are involved. And not only is the confrontation there between America and Russia direct, it is naval and not military.

Thus, America has been pledged to defend a Europe that has not been in danger of a Russian attack, while Europe has been doing very well by dealing directly with Russia. America's continued diversion of financial strength to anachronistic military subsidies for European creditors merely delays America's efforts to find the billions needed to catch up with the commanding position Russia has won in the sea race.

The contemporary history of America's shoe industry illustrates the consequences of the subordination of America's economic bargaining power to her foreign military commitments. America's overextended foreign military stance has compelled her again and again to navigate between domestic pressures to move towards import agreements and international pressures to keep them voluntary—that is, toothless tokens. Granted, in isolated instances—and in response to political muscle—Washington has acknowledged import peril points past which a basic industry would qualify for relief. In 1971 voluntary agreements were negotiated to limit textile imports to 8 percent of the domestic market; while in the same year steel imports were cut successively from 16 percent to 11 percent of the domestic market.

With characteristic inconsistency, however, the administration tolerated a rise in shoe imports accounting for more than 37 percent of domestic sales. By January 1972, import penetration in the industry had reached an all-time high, equaling more than 66 percent of domestic production. The demoralized shoe manufacturers and unions petitioned Washington for protection comparable to what the steel and textile industries had been granted. But they ran into a barrage of mumbo jumbo.

An administration dedicated to "full employment" found nothing alarming about 219 factory shutdowns in the past three years or 100,000 shoe workers added to the army of unemployed—both as a direct result of imports. Nor did they heed irrefutable warnings of a bulge in the cost-of-living index due to higher shoe prices forced by the increased price of raw materials. Thanks to its indulgence of the country's cattlemen and packers, the Price Commission had blinked its eyes at a hide price increase of 130 percent between August 13, 1971, and May 31, 1972.

Powers committed to economic survival are seldom prepared to tolerate, much less promote, unrestrained exports of their essential raw materials at the expense of their basic domestic industries. Yet the Department of Commerce pointed with pride to the increased outflow of hides inflated in worth to approximately $100 million; while the more-than-offsetting imports of shoes and leather products adding up to $800 million were dismissed as irrelevant. All of this at the very time that Treasury Secretary Connally was tearing a passion to tatters because he had been charged five dollars for eggs Benedict in an East Side Manhattan hotel.

America's shoe industry had been sacrificed as a hostage for one of America's foreign military commitments. Spain had spearheaded the move responsible for the administration's immobilization in this sensitive area of pocketbook politics. Not only had she been permitted to preempt more than 11 percent of the lucrative import market; Spain's workhorse wage rates had subsidized her ability to bid up the export prices of American hides. General Franco—no neophyte at the game our lobbying allies have learned to play with America's subsidy dollars—had served notice on Kissinger that any restrictions on the access of low-cost Spanish shoes to the American market would be countered with complete restrictions on the access of America's Mediterranean fleet to its high-cost, special-purpose Spanish base.

Nixon's favorite razzle-dazzle football play explains the fumble which turned his bold effort to score abroad into a rout on his own goal line. For it was literally the end-around play that forced his surrender. His foreign opposition mounted what in football terms is called a triple-threat counteroffensive. Politically, his foreign adversaries at the bargaining table in Europe were clients. Economically, they were competitors. Financially, they were creditors.

Nixon's power play was intended to put European nations on the defensive economically in their capacity as competitors. Their first response as creditors was to aim a sharp straight buck against the weakened line defending the dollar. But they quickly turned this simple play into a more complicated end-around play in their capacity as clients of the pax Americana. They threatened him with the loss of face that would follow from Europe's renegotiation of their status as an "American protectorate." Nixon buckled under their threats and surrendered the surcharge.

But the best that could be said about any and all international emergency expedients adopted was that they would work as well as, and no better than, the domestic emergency expedients packaged with them. If—and only if!—the domestic emergency measures got the American economy moving in the right direction again, and in time to prevent the American economy from being pushed in the wrong direction, the international expedients would be helpful. Failure of the domestic part of the program was bound to spell disaster for its international ingredients. The worst to be feared was that the President's dramatic exercise in "doing something" would not work out as the catalyst of recovery inside the American economy; and that, therefore, America's recession would put the foreign dollar-holding powers in need of a competitive devaluation of their own.

Export price-cutting by Germany and Japan scarcely went with confidence in the stability of the newly devalued dollar. But the other side of the coin from devaluation pressures on the dollar creditor countries, and suspicion of the devalued dollar, was quickly reflected in the continued strength of the gold market. Meanwhile, although the danger of protectionism that the import surcharge provoked was a false alarm, the failure of the economy that followed from its surrender made protectionism a real threat.

A double demonstration on the part of the government had been required to get the domestic economy moving again. The first called for the government to show the American business buyer and the members of the work force—whose families set consumer spending trends—that it meant to get foreign competition off his back and, therefore, off theirs. The second awaited a return of confidence on the part of business in the stability of its costs. This called for getting labor off the back of business.

Nixon's August 15 answer to the controversy on the domestic front was to declare a wage-price freeze. It was a case of too much, too soon. While emergency controls in time of war are a necessary evil, they were a dubious experiment in time of peace. Nixon himself was more than normally candid in acknowledging his jeopardy in imposing them. He admitted that he would have been worried if anyone less committed than himself to free enterprise had imposed them.

However, once committed to the freeze, Nixon blundered in putting a ninety-day time limit on it. The moment he did, he invited speculation on what he would do on the ninety-first day. Only two courses of action would be open to him: extend the unsustainable freeze, or open loopholes in it. In its brief ninety-day lifetime, the cure proved worse than the complaint. Invocation of the freeze as the ultimate weapon made a Phase Two retreat to controls inevitable.

The impact of controls under the aegis of the Pay Board and the Price Commission only served to confirm the slump in the domestic economy. Each new sign of break-down in the new system signaled a confirmation for the holdback in consumer spending. Labor's loss of confidence in its own wage gains had helped bring on the crisis, and labor's withholding of confidence in the controls that promised to make its money worth more deepened the crisis. The economists had reckoned without this backlash of no-confidence on the part of labor. They had jumped to the conclusion that, because the government had moved, the economy would.

The slot machine manned by the Pay Board during Phase Two's ill-fated tenure put the stamp of regulatory approval on spiraling costs. But a stretch-out of the time span of existing union contracts is the way to negotiate a moratorium on their escalation provisions. A two-phase trade-off had been the obvious answer. The first step would have swapped job security against import competition. The second, negotiated on the basis of the first, would have traded a return to overtime against a temporary holiday in wage rates. The double freeze on import volume and on the labor cost push would have catalyzed the business buyer. The resultant return to overtime would have compensated labor for agreeing to a pause in the wage-rate spiral. After all, the wage-rate spiral had all along been labor's answer to the loss of overtime, to the shrinkage in the work week, and to the rising chanciness of steady employment.

The fiscal side of Nixon's New Economic Program was its third and final salient feature. It was the feature on which he put least emphasis, yet it was the decisive one. Two chairmen, Mills and Burns, had combined to call on the administration to switch its reliance from government spending to business investment as the prime mover in the economy. Acknowledging the political force of the spend-less, tax-less approach, Nixon called for reactivation of the investment tax credit.

While the wage-price freeze had been a case of too much too soon, Nixon's call for reactivation of the investment tax credit was too little too late. The cost inflation legalized in Phase Two and the profit squeeze on labor-intensive industries reflected in the sag of the product price structure (as distinguished from the continued inflation of the cost of services) confirmed this judgment.

The need for reactivation of the investment tax credit early in 1971 was indeed much greater than the need for its original adoption in 1962. So was the further need for supporting tax credits (notably for job training and child care). But the stagflation in the economy had passed the point at which meaningful new hope could be held for the willingness or ability of business to use the investment tax credit. After all, no company in the entire tax-paying system was without its equivalent of RCA's computer catastrophe. Taking RCA as the horrible example proving the rule, what incentive would it have to put out hard new dollars to buy new tax credits so long as it remained rich in tax write-offs on bad old investments, poor in money-good customers and saddled with surplus facilities?

The other portion of Nixon's tax-less program was just as meaningless. It did indeed provide nominal tax concessions to the lowest bracket of individual taxpayers. But for the representative cross-section of individual taxpayers, the promise of relief turned into the shock of revolt when the 1972 withholding tax schedules went into effect. The only countable reductions were in take-home pay. Withholding tax rates were up, especially on the so-called popular middle brackets.

An unpublicized comedy of errors had left the government in urgent need of passing this phony "tax cut" bill, and in even more urgent need of turning it by Executive order into an actual tax increase. Unbelievable though it may seem, the Treasury had been guilty of a full-fledged boner in printing and distributing the 1970 withholding tax tables for 1971 income. Underwithholding had been the result, and a brutal catch-up levy would have been the consequence if the "tax cut" had not been passed to offset it.

A simultaneous day of reckoning would have been in order for corporate taxpayers, whose depreciation charge-offs had also been understated and whose 1971 tax accruals were exposing them to a costly catch-up. On the merits, the "trickle down" benefits from the rate cuts in the tax-less part of the New Economic Program were never meant to be more than tokens. To the extent that they were, they never added up to more than offsets against scheduled increases.

A bookkeeping "wash" was the cynical purpose of the "tax cut" bill presented to Congress. Raising more cash remained its problem after its showcase operation had been completed. Overwithholding by decree and without even the formalities of discussion with Congress was its solution.

The arbitrary switch of an advertised tax cut into an extralegal tax increase imposed a more cynical and high-handed White House dictate over Congress than had been perpetrated in the escalation of the Vietnam war. At least Johnson had acknowledged the Constitutional formalities by calling for the Tonkin Gulf resolution. Nixon had no comparable procedural fig leaf to hide behind when a tax cut passed by Congress and approved by him was transmogrified by Executive fiat into a tax increase. The operation represented an intellectual crime against the hallowed Keynesian creed to which Nixon had confessed his conversion. His acquired political Keynesianism had committed him to stimulate the economy by draining fewer dollars out of the spending stream. His inherited fiscal bankruptcy had forced him to load a $4 billion tax increase on it.

Thus, the tax-less portion of the fiscal thrust of the President's New Economic Program was meaningless as a spur to the crisis of stagflation in the tax-paying economy. Its spend-less promise was never meant to be meaningful for the budget crisis in the tax-collecting economy.

While the President had addressed himself, however inadequately, to the source of the fiscal crisis in the private economy, his emergency program showed but the slightest of concern for the fiscal crisis in the public economy. The proposed $5 billion cut in federal spending was a dead letter before the intragovernmental mail carrying the President's formal proposals ever reached Congress.

The progress of the new fiscal year into Phase Two found the government admitting crisis and claiming that the deficit measuring it would work out as the economy's last, best hope of recovery. All along, the administration had been estimating a mere $23 billion deficit in the budget. The onset of the first year of emergency witnessed an admitted inflation of the federal deficit to $28 billion and led to a significant quarrel inside Nixon's official family.

Treasury Secretary Connally was at odds with the White House and under pressure from his Democratic friends to resign as an act of political warfare against Nixon. Instead, the tactic on which he settled was to leak word that the projected budget deficit would be not $28 billion, but a whopping $38 billion. By the time 1972's political campaign opened later in the spring, the skirmish was over and Connally was running for the Vice Presidential nomination. He celebrated the amnesty he negotiated with the White House with a dramatic announcement: the budget deficit was back down to under $30 billion and he was, therefore, about to start paying down the national debt.

Overwithholding (albeit subject to massive refunds in 1973) accounted in part for the reduction in federal borrowing requirements. The improvement in the economy produced another bonus: tax collections on higher earnings never fail to yield a rich and quick dividend to the Treasury. Chairman Herbert Stein, of the Council of Economic Advisers, revealed a third source when he admitted that pushing new spending commitments out into the money stream took more time and trouble than he had ever realized.

Nevertheless, interest rates did not come down with these official guesstimates of the Treasury's reduced borrowing needs. The credit markets responded to a drop in the official federal deficit to below $30 billion—a level that had originally put short-term interest rates up—by putting them up still higher.

Long-term rates discounted the reassuring news too. However susceptible the stock market still was to manipulation by the administration's newsmaking apparatus, the bond market had learned the hard way to defend itself against the inflationary dynamite loaded into the federal borrowing operation. Sensitized to the sustained inflationary thrust built into the momentum of deficit financing, the bond market reckoned with the federal deficit arithmetic on a two-year span. The official disclosure that the Treasury's borrowing needs would be less than expected for fiscal 1973 left it fearful that the borrowing load for fiscal 1974 would be greater than expected.

The bond market had also learned to look past the rise and fall of budgeted borrowings and to anticipate a constant increase in the level of "debudgeted" borrowings by the federal agencies underwritten by the Treasury. To take the most conspicuous example, Treasury-guaranteed borrowings on the scale of something like $12 billion a year were required to sustain the role played by federal housing operations in assuring a housing start level of 2½ million a year. To take another, Nixon's 1972 travels obligated the Export-Import Bank to invoke the full faith and credit of the United States in support of a step-up in its long-term borrowings.

But whether the news stream reported an uptick or a downtick in the level of the federal deficit, its "normalization" at a traditionally unacceptable level resolved the chicken-and-egg quandary about the deficit and the economy. Contrary to the claims of the "new economics," the slippage in the economy had been the cause of the run-up in the deficit. Moreover, while the run-up in the deficit had failed to correct the shrinkage in the economy, the most moderate start towards a recovery in the economy was enough to bring a quick drop in the deficit.

The rest is now history—specifically, the history of the

failure that was unthinkable in the election year whose prosperity was guaranteed to be bankable. Leads and lags describe more than the statistical record of recovery and recessionary symptoms. The economy and its markets work in the same way leadership works in the forging of great events. Recoveries take hold when sectors of the economy provide leadership which lasts long enough to start a follow-through reaction among laggard sectors. Contrariwise, recoveries peter out into false starts when the sectors which spurt run out of steam before laggard sectors are caught up in their wake.

Leadership for the American economy now awaits a response more commanding than the performance of any industry or group of industries can provide. Only the White House can. Its failure to provide the leadership that was wanted in the crisis of 1971 sentenced the economy to flounder in a series of false starts until the leadership gap is closed at the top managerial level.

Three sectors of the American economy spurted in 1971—automotive, residential building, and the stock market. The automotive and housing booms told the same story. The stock market told a story of its own. Divergence was the dominant characteristic of the auto and housing boom. Never before had both these major fabricators of primary products run at record levels while their suppliers—of steel, aluminum, brass, glass, rubber, chemicals, and textiles—stagnated in a stubborn slump.

This divergence posed the 1972 dollar question for the economy: Would the auto and housing recovery last long enough to force a revival of business buying and, therefore, of activity and employment in the primary industries which supplied both user sectors that connect pri-

mary production with the consumer? The surrender of
the surcharge answered the question with a dismaying
"No"—to Nixon's surprise. His surprise was built into his
priorities.

Nixon never connected the economic side of his problem with the diplomatic and always assumed that optimistic GNP projections represented realistic trends in the
trend-making sectors of the economy. Therefore, his fear
of losing face in his dealings with his foreign client creditors distracted him from his jeopardy of losing position
inside his domestic power base to his foreign competitors.

Meanwhile, the story of its own the stock market told
in 1971 and 1972 documented its peculiar nature. For the
stock market goes with present money conditions, and it
anticipates future business conditions. In 1971, money
conditions were easy; and business conditions looked
good for 1972 "because Nixon has to get reelected."
Moreover, foreign buying was touted as guaranteeing a
markup and a bailout to any and all Americans beating it
to the sell side of the market. Not until after the market
made new highs for volume, but failed to translate them
into new highs for the leading averages, did the seesaw
tilt the other way. Moreover, just when higher interest
rates made money conditions less attractive to investors,
lower activity rates made business conditions more uncer-
tain, too—not least thanks to the slump in the overseas
economies where the best companies had been recording
the most dynamic gains for the most glamorous stocks.
Just when the dollar devaluation deal began to come unstuck, the dollar devaluation rally came unstuck with it.

The stock market had started out being unrealistic in
identifying the world monetary crisis as the main threat

to its stability. It turned out to be realistic when the failure of the American economy to normalize precluded the ability of the international currency rearrangement to work. The failure of the world economy to stabilize was at once the consequence of the setbacks already suffered and the setbacks still to come.

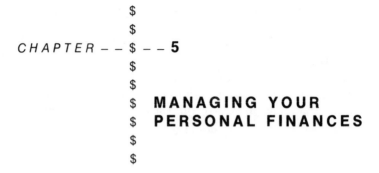

CHAPTER – – $ – – **5**

MANAGING YOUR PERSONAL FINANCES

"**T**he government will manage," has been accepted as the first article of faith for every knowledgeable American family and business during the generation since the last depression. "It can never happen again," has been the rule of the money road unquestionably accepted by all but a frightened fringe of American money-users. Americans have felt free to spend more, to borrow more, and to expect more because they have felt confident of having more to make do with. Bullishness was the unquestioning premise of the affluent period. Clearly, however, it has now ended. No doubt a cultural lag still explains both the reluctance to write it off and the expectation that it will return. The governing premise of the affluent era trusted Washington's power over money—on two counts: either to keep everyone making it; or, even more profitable in slow years, to insure everyone against running out of it.

Back before the government undertook to play Big Uncle for everyone, people used to talk about laying aside a reserve for a rainy day. Now that the government has got all mixed up between giving money to its customers and getting money from them, every day has begun to rain trouble. The fiasco the government has made of its own budgeting is putting the private customers for its services, from whom it gets its money, on notice to put personal prudence first in managing their own personal family and business budgeting.

A saying in vogue since postal service began to deteriorate—"The bills come in promptly, only the checks don't"—is applicable. For it suggests the prudence of considering the cost side of the family budget before the income side. Inflation on the cost side has left everyone worrying because each dollar is buying less. Now controls are hitting everyone with a new worry: that everyone will be having fewer dollars with which to buy less.

Emergency controls go with emergency taxes. Phases One and Two may not have cut costs, but upcoming emergency taxes can be trusted to cut income. For the duration of the siege of money trouble, prudent budgeters —having already stopped banking on hopes of higher pretax income—will reckon on higher taxes taking a big new bite out of their checkbooks.

But while the cost of living is continuing to inflate, the product mix of inflation is changing. A paradox—complicated on the surface, but simple from the vantage point of business and family budgeting—explains it. The prices of goods have started to go down; and the pressure on producers to move goods is driving them down further by the day. But the cost of services is going up. Businesses with products to sell are being forced to offer bargains. Nevertheless, getting services rendered is costing more; and the people rendering these services—from governments to repair men—still feel free to make them cost even more.

The era of affluence has complicated the job of drawing a practical dividing line between goods and services. Increasingly, goods are packaged to include services. The current uptrend in food prices—accelerated by a worldwide shortage of both grain and meat—offers an example. Today's competitively high prices to food producers, both cattlemen and farmers—combined with service add-ons for processing, packaging, and transportation —are putting everyone who wants to save any money on notice to include food costs in their list of budgeting priorities.

The most common services are physical labor, repairs, transportation, meals, fees, rent, interest, and insurance— with taxes for the services government renders adding the biggest toll on the cost of living, of dying, and of doing business in between.

When the inflation of goods prices first turned into an inflation of service costs, the federal government in Washington was still focusing its attention on possible tax cuts. Only local governments, aware that their tax bases had been cut, raised their service charges. Now the federal government is set to pace the next round of inflated service costs.

The most common fallacy in the way people talk about inflation is expressed in the confusion between the prices of goods and the cost of living. This confusion blurred the point of the speech President Nixon made when he introduced Phase Two. He pointed to the drop in prices for goods as proof of progress against inflation (as if the fact of Phase Two did not institutionalize a victory for it). He forgot that more people spend more money on services than on goods. As a matter of fact, the government itself spends a higher portion of each dollar on services, and a smaller portion on goods, than any other entity in the economy. Even hospitals, which are continuous buyers of goods—all the way from paper-and-string items to expensive equipment—spend something like 80 cents of every dollar for services and only 20 cents for tangibles.

The most timely place to begin budgeting for the emergency is to go over the last six months of checkbook entries in a systematic effort to tabulate your own cost-of-living product mix as between goods and services. You will be surprised by the high claim on your dollar drain being accounted for by payments leaving you nothing tangible in return. Repairs are an exception—provided the repairs make your cars, appliances, furniture and fixtures work, instead of putting them in need of still more repairs. Learn to be critical of spending which seems to buy goods but on scrutiny turns out to buy services packaged into goods.

The new boom in two old businesses shows that lifestyle changes are being made by a great many families with sharp pencils and willing hands who have caught on to the costly extent to which expensive services have been packaged into cheap goods, inflating their cost. Home sewing—as old a business as any—is accounting for the first such boom. And camping out is responsible for shortages in equipment while hotel and motel rooms are going begging.

Do-it-yourself is the name of the game which balances the falling cost of goods against the rising cost of services. More and more people are staying even or getting ahead by playing it—all the way from food and clothing to shelter and recreation. (Witness, for example, the many well-to-do families moving into homes they can run themselves.) And nowadays every family determined to make sense out of its dollar problems will do well to calculate its goods /services product mix in order to balance bargains in the buying of goods against the toll taken by the continuing inflation in the cost of services.

The fact is that the charges for getting things done are rising faster than bargain price tags are appearing on goods. The price of a refrigerator, to take one of any number of conspicuous examples of old luxuries which are new necessities, is just about the same as it was back in the 1950s. Only the cost of moving and repairing it, or buying it on time—and, of course, paying the gas or electricity bill for it—has been inflated. The enormous improvement in the product does not show on the price tag —including more power delivered in a smaller box able to do more work in a smaller kitchen. But the cost of the services involved in using it hurts in the pocketbook.

The increasing bargain-mindedness of the representative consumer—all the way from the top income brackets to the bottom—is not enough to build defenses against cost inflation. Buying marked-down goods will not help so long as paying for marked-up services preempts more than half of the family's budget. Nor is this same bargain-mindedness among consumers buying any insurance against income deflation. On the contrary. The downgrading of consumer preferences to "mini" models, their holdback until bargains are offered, and their switch to import brands, is accentuating the earnings squeeze on the manufacturers of goods. But manufacturers are also employers. And the backlash from the threat to corporate earnings is measured by the realistic spread of insecurity for family earnings.

Everything ever said by the familiar complaint "It

never rains but it pours" applies to the coincidence which turned consumers to bargain-mindedness at the peak of a generation-old cycle which left them amply stocked with goods of all kinds; and, worse still, at the start of a cycle which switched their priorities away from goods or left them tolerating goods as a necessary evil. The revulsion against pollution was only a part of it, although it is true that the "maxi" consumer investment goods, in premium demand during the heyday of affluence, netted the biggest profit margins to producers. The revulsion from the high cost of services required to use and repair big homes, big cars, and big appliances reinforced the new trend.

The people who read *What Shall I Do With My Money?*, and followed its simple guidelines, have cash and have been accumulating more of it. They are ready and able to take advantage of the bargains being offered for goods. They can do so without eating up their savings reserves or their investment programs. Nor are they being forced into getting caught short with a car that is no longer worth repairing or with a home that has missed its market.

These people have been observing the three fundamental rules formulated in Chapter II of *What Shall I Do With My Money?* The first calls for spending no more than 25 percent of net post-tax income for shelter— whether for rent or for the after-tax cost of servicing a mortgage.

The second rule calls for holding in a savings reserve at least 10 percent of one year's pre-tax income (earned plus unearned)—except (and this exception is just as important as the underlying rule) for families whose members may either have health problems or be losing health insurance coverage with their jobs. A workable alternative, aimed at protecting people with higher incomes and/or reserves of capital against oversaving and underinvesting, is to keep a savings reserve equivalent to six months living costs.

Don't be misled into the easy assumption that the new emergency control system ordered August 15 justified any relaxation of the 10 percent saving rule. On the contrary, controls multiply uncertainties; and the uncertainties brought on by the August 15 regulations, multiplied by their subsequent amendments, argue for saving more and not less.

The third rule recognizes life insurance as a second priority cost-of-living budget item (right after food, clothing, and shelter), and sets a policy-owning target of straight life equal to five years worth of pre-tax earned income plus at least the first five years worth of any mortgage and/or short-term debt. No single recommendation is more constructive and more universally applicable than the recommendation to maximize life insurance coverage. It may hurt in the beginning but it will help every family long before the finish. Moreover, the earlier any family starts buying its insurance, the bigger the bargain it will buy in the cost of the basic protection it pays for. Last but not least, believe it or not, insurance is still exempt from the long list of services whose costs are steadily rising. It's remaining every bit the bargain it has been all during the entire inflation.

Until the minimum insurance target has been met, it is prudent to defer lower priority claims on the family budget. Of course, by taking full advantage of the protection available through a group plan, individual requirements can be minimized—that is, provided the employee can be sure of not winding up unemployed and uninsured.

Remember that insurance paid for through a company plan is purchased with pre-tax dollars that represent a partial write-off for the company; while individuals pay for insurance with after-tax dollars. Companies also pay lower premiums since they are figured at a wholesale rate. Almost all group insurance plans provide only term coverage, although some do offer group permanent insurance. The latter coverage combines term and straight life insurance, with the employer paying for the term insurance and the employee paying the difference—thereby accruing some equity or cash reserve. In any case, it is important in calculating insurance needs not to confuse insurance with either savings or investment but, instead, to use it to buy protection sufficient to meet the ongoing financial needs of dependent beneficiaries.

Life insurance policies fall into three categories. Taking them in reverse order of economic utility, endowment policies are first; ordinary ("cash value") life policies are second; and term policies are third.

Endowment policies are the least economic because they invite the policy owner to buy a compromise between insurance and investment. As so often happens with compromises, this one buys the short end of both deals. It represents the highest cost of insurance and the lowest return on investment. Most insurance companies are practical enough to recognize the needs as well as the sophistication of their customers and, therefore, they are letting the endowment policy go the way of the dinosaur.

Ordinary "cash value" insurance represents a higher-cost way of buying protection than term insurance. But it has offsetting advantages that make it well worth the difference for a great many different groups of people in need of protection. One such group consists of younger people. The lower premium available to them gives them a lifelong bargain, free from any problems or costs connected with rights of renewal. Another group consists of people lacking confidence in their disciplined ability to budget for cost-of-living priorities. They recognize their need to live free from the temptation to let a term insurance policy lapse instead of exercising their right of renewal. Ordinary (cash value) life policies guarantee erratic budgeters the right to borrow their premiums against accrued cash reserves during lean years.

A third group consists of resourceful money-users interested in building up a cheap and sure source of borrowing power, subject neither to credit scrutiny nor to repayment requirements. Owners of cash value life insurance buy with their premiums a constant right to generate 5 percent money for as long as they want it during credit squeezes when money may cost twice as much and carry onerous conditions with it.

The rate at which cash values build up—after three years of premiums have been paid—with subsequent premiums paid is stipulated in all ordinary life contracts. Just as endowment policies offer the most uneconomic combination of insurance and investment, so ordinary cash value life insurance represents an economic combination of life and credit insurance. And it best fulfills the basic service of insurance: lifetime protection at a pre-established cost.

This said, the fact remains that in the relations between insurance policyholders and insurance companies, as in the relationship between taxpayers and their government, nothing is free. Higher cost, ordinary cash value life insurance buys more protection than term insurance. Therefore, its cost is inescapably higher—enough higher to provide the cash reserve for which the policyholder pays. The cost of providing the service underwritten in this cash reserve varies from company to company. Herbert S. Denenberg, Pennsylvania's Commissioner of Insurance, called dramatic attention to these variations in his April 1972 Shopper's Guide to Life Insurance. His cost analysis of straight life insurance reveals startling discrepancies. For instance, the same protection purchased from one company is provided by another for one-third the cost. The difference in cost represents the competitive spread between companies.

The third form of life insurance is term insurance. The policyholder buys nothing but protection against death for the term stipulated. Almost without exception, term insurance policies have no cash value. Because they are used up with each passing day, they can be bought at substantially lower rates than straight life. Coverage is for a specified period of time—as with automobile, fire, theft, and hospitalization insurance.

A term policy can provide insurance for one year or, alternatively, up to and beyond age seventy. Coverage can be renewable or non-renewable. Non-renewable term insurance requires that the policyholder first re-apply for coverage and then meet stipulated health standards. This means that the young and healthy buyer of non-renewable term insurance is gambling on the risk of losing that protection—or paying exorbitant premiums for it—at a time when a life insurance medical examination may be difficult to pass. Renewable term insurance is renewed automatically with no physical examination. In each case, premiums are figured on an escalated basis—automatically for renewable, and at the time of renewal for non-renewable.

Where the need is for current protection only, the money saved by relying on term instead of ordinary life insurance can be freed for more profitable investment elsewhere. An obvious situation is one in which the owner of an ordinary life insurance policy is making a loan. A term insurance policy adds no more than a nominal fraction to the cost of the loan and will protect the borrower's estate against the loss of protection in the event of death before the loan is paid. Some lenders provide this accommodation at the wholesale rate as part of the credit package they offer.

Another situation calling for the use of term insurance occurs when there is need for a considerable amount of protection—perhaps to underwrite the education of children—and the cost of straight life insurance is far in excess of realistic family budgeting. By purchasing term insurance, the money saved is available to meet current budgeting priorities.

In case of disability, one important provision is usually structured into the premiums for both straight life and term policies. It guarantees that the policy remains in force while the obligation to pay premiums is automatically suspended for the duration of such disability. If this provision is not part of your coverage it can be included for a nominal amount.

The common denominator in the purchase of all insurance is the insurance agent who sells the policy. You can buy a home—or a used car or a block of stock or a business—directly from someone you know. You cannot buy a life insurance policy from any company without dealing with one of its agents. (Small SBLI policies offered by some savings banks are a minor exception; and so are "per trip" policies merchandised at airports.)

The way to deal with the life insurance agent or agents soliciting your business is, first, to define your needs relative to your means and, then, to ask for a comparison in cost and benefits with those offered by their competitors.

Insurance policy sales are soaring to new highs. So is the premium income of the life insurance industry. The record rate at which new insurance policies are bought and sold, and at which old policies are being paid up, attests to the enormous size and continuous growth of the reservoir of savings owned by the American people. The rising pressure on the life insurance industry to meet cost competition attests to the new determination and ability of consumers to get as much as their dollar can buy. After all, lower premiums can buy more insurance. And the more insurance you do buy, the better off you and your beneficiaries will be.

It is no exaggeration to say that the country's life insurance companies comprise the one major industry insured against the ravages of cost inflation. The life insurance companies are not being burdened by higher costs. But they are benefiting from the higher flow of income—both from policy premiums and from their investments—resulting from higher costs. Insurance companies are also benefiting from the impressive increase in everyone's life expectancy. This enables them to count on having the use of the policyholders' premium payments for a longer time span and to count on deferring the settlements due on death.

Thanks to this exception, most buyers of ordinary life insurance are getting a bargain, while the country's life insurance companies are in better financial shape than ever —and that's going some. More than incidentally, this helps explain why the continuing emergency, although it spells money trouble for so many people, is not going to see policyholders' savings lost or their protection jeopardized.

A word is in order here on pension plans, for they offer retirement planning opportunities for an increasing number of families. But a dismayingly large number of families have been shocked to discover in recent years that participation in pension plans is no substitute for life insurance, for savings, and for systematic investment. A study conducted by a subcommittee of the Senate Committee on Labor and Public Welfare—under the auspices of its chairman, Senator Harrison A. Williams, Jr., of New Jersey—has shown conclusively that the overwhelming majority of participants in pension plans have been forfeiting their rights instead of cashing in on them. Another disturbingly large number of pension plan participants were never given vested rights in such plans.

The fact that forfeitures were suffered by millions of employees during years when payrolls were expanding suggests that forfeitures will be even more widespread now that the pressure is on employers to shrink their work forces. Salaried employees are particularly vulnerable to the drive to cut overhead costs. But hourly workers are correspondingly vulnerable to the provision written into union contracts that the first to be hired are the first to be fired: most pension plans set minimum periods of service, like fifteen or even twenty-five years, as a qualification for receiving retirement pension benefits.

Exposure to forfeiture is by no means limited to the employees of fly-by-night operators or smaller companies. The Senate Committee on Labor and Public Welfare pointed up this hazard in its study of some 1500 pension plans. A typical example cited in this study is the pension plan of a large oil company that provides for 50 percent vesting after fifteen years, with vesting increased at 5 percent each year thereafter until there is 100 percent vesting after twenty-five years. But of the 105,000 persons who have participated in the plan since 1950, less than 8,500 retired with full benefits. More than 61,000 left with no benefits—3,680 of them with more than ten years of service and 13,430 with more than five years of service.

In the case of a large communications company with approximately 57,000 employees, its pension plan had no vesting provisions until 1969. The plan now provides full vesting at age forty with fifteen years of service. Nevertheless, of the 152,028 persons participating in the plan since 1966, 108,035 left with no benefits. Of that number, 2,284 left after more than fifteen years of service, while 4,592 had been employed more than ten years, and 8,778 more than five years.

It is reassuring to reflect that such situations may prove to be temporary. Legislation sponsored by Senator Jacob K. Javits of New York, would provide a remedy. The thrust of the bill he has introduced is to establish minimum standards for vesting and funding; to establish a pension plan reinsurance program; to provide for the "portability" of pension fund credits; and to sharpen present pension fund disclosure obligations. Federal regulation of minimum funding requirements will uncover hair-curling deficiencies even before retirement benefits are liberalized, and even without a stock market break.

Assuring retirement pension benefits for the millions of employees now forfeiting them would mean greater security for the retired, but greater employment and investment insecurity. For increased funding requirements would sharpen the profit squeeze on employers, making investment in their securities more chancy. Subjecting pension funds to rules comparable to those governing mutual funds, and to a stringent new deal on reporting their operations to their beneficiaries and to the regulatory authorities, would force a massive readjustment in the stock market. So would the thrust of the limitations now to be anticipated on employers' investment and speculative operations.

Until this protective legislation now belatedly under consideration does change the rules governing the operation of pension plans, it behooves all employees to get clear as to whether they can count on taking more than their severance pay with them when they leave.

Q: What do you think is the most workable form for setting up a family budget?

Mr. W. D. (Tulsa, Oklahoma)

A: Good family budgeting is bounded by a ceiling over rent—or over the cost of shelter (rent is the term for it, whether you are a tenant or a homeowner)—and a floor under savings. The absolute maximum for any family working for a living to spend on housing is 25 percent of total take-home pay. The bare minimum to squirrel away for a rainy day is 10 percent of annual take-home pay—before taxes and including income budgeted for rent—or a sum sufficient to cover six months' living expenses.

Begin by calculating your family health costs for the last five years, separating the unpredictable, recurring sick bills everyone has, from the predictable nonrecurring ones (such as childbirth). Then look back over the last five years, with a view to looking forward to determine whether changes in your neighborhood and new family plans may persuade you to move in the next five years. If you think you won't want, or need, to move, estimate how much your home will eat up in increased repairs and taxes—including maintenance and, of course, mortgage debt. Be sure to balance your expectations for higher earnings against the higher education expenses you can anticipate. An increasing number of families are learning to break even on living expenses and family obligations with what the head of the household earns, while relying on the wife's going to work to build up savings reserves and to earn the makings of an investment program.

Q: Again and again, you refer to the difference between savings and investment money as they relate to an individual. Could you expand on this further by defining the difference for me?

Mr. C. B. (Hinsdale, Illinois)

A: The purpose of savings is not only to earn a minimal return but, more importantly, to build a close-to-cash emergency reserve—that is, not to make money, but to have money. Saving comes first for those trying to accumulate money—first, for security and, then, for investment. Neither gain nor return is the standard for measuring what savings will do for you; protection plus ready access to ready money is. Investment is for those who have money—enough to tide them over emergencies.

Investment assumes the availability of ready money to put to work over a period of time—without any pressure to produce a quick payback. Again and again, due to unbudgeted needs for cash, sound investments come under pressure of forced liquidation before they can work out. The way to insure against this is to budget a savings target equal to six months' living expenses before starting to invest. After the savings reserve test has been met, keep saving at the same rate, earmarking everything over your basic savings reserve for investment. Families with health problems need still bigger cash reserves. Families meeting this standard, but burdened with education financing problems, will do well to finance their youngsters' education before trying to make money, build capital, or buy unearned income for themselves.

Q: I read your column but seldom see any advice for the guy who makes $12,000 or less. How about some advice for the little guy?

Mr. W. M. (Wood Dale, Illinois)

A: You haven't read it often enough. If you had, you would see that I begin by advising him to put his romantic trust in girls wanting and able to work too, and who learn how to make sense with their money as well as dollars from their skills. The littler any guy is, the surer he and his girl can be that they will not make out against inflation and job insecurity with only one of them willing and able to work.

Q: I am a married college student with around $4,000 in savings which I would like to invest. The stock market seems to be out of the question. What about putting my money in a 5 percent Swiss franc account in a Swiss bank? The risks seem to be few, and it seems like the best way to get good exchange rates while abroad.

Mr. J. B. (Chicago, Illinois)

A: You are dead right that the stock market is out of the question—but not because it is so risky now. Even if it were less risky, it would not offer a prudent use for your $4,000 savings. No one with this little can hope to do as well in the stock market as in a savings account without running the risk of losing it all. In your circumstances, only a savings objective is appropriate. With your family obligations, and with your present earning power, you need an emergency fund in liquid form. Life insurance, not investment, is your next priority.

The worst way to continue saving would be to fall for the allure of a Swiss franc savings account. The game you would then be playing is one of currency speculation, which is at the opposite end of the money-using spectrum from savings. As a practical matter, Swiss banks are no longer paying interest on new, foreign accounts. Beyond this, if matters of theory interest you as well, the European currencies are now getting overvalued; so that devaluation for them is becoming a danger too. True, the Swiss franc would be the last European currency to run this risk. Nevertheless, an international money crisis is no place for innocents abroad.

Q: We are in our early thirties with two children under ten years of age. We have $20,000 paid-up life insurance. Our problem is that we are unable to make ends meet—much less savings targets—on my husband's $15,000-a-year income. We seem to be constantly falling behind and want to know what kind of planning you think we can adopt.

Mrs. J. L. (Pittsburgh, Pennsylvania)

A: Why don't you go to work? I suspect that your family money problem results from backward-looking assumptions about woman's place being in the home. No longer can the average American family assume the responsibilities for its youngsters' education with just the husband-father working. Clinging to this assumption is now a passport to family budget trouble.

Either the wife-mother is going to go to work or families' expectations and standards of living are going to give. Admittedly, the absence of children's day centers, operating under acceptable standards, is a major socio-economic obstacle to women in your age bracket going to work—or back to work—and making ends meet with any plus to spare.

Nevertheless, I think that the answer to your budgeting problem is to be found in what the youngsters call "a life-style" problem.

As my wife, Elizabeth Janeway, explained in her definitive book *Man's World, Woman's Place,* more than half the women of childbearing age in America are now employed. The rise of part-time employment for mothers is running neck-and-neck with the full-time entry of women into the labor force as the most dynamic single plus in American economic society. You will find that getting a part-time job will get you into the swim socially while helping you and your family to keep your heads above water economically.

Q: I am a CPA, employed by a major oil company. My wife and I are both forty-eight. Both of us have been burdened by heavy, continuous obligations to aging invalid parents and, consequently, our ability to save has been hampered in spite of heavy step-ups in my salary of $17,500. My wife worked as a medical secretary when we were first married, but both of us figured that we would be ahead of the game by saving on nurses instead of paying them with money she might otherwise be earning.

Our problem centers on our insurance. We have a $40,000 endowment policy. In addition, I have ten years' seniority with my company. After another ten, I will qualify for a retirement pension. Its size would of course depend on further pay increases I might get in the next ten years. Meanwhile, for the duration of our obligations to our parents, we are not likely to have any margin to save. Do you think we would do better to take out a loan on our endowment policy and begin to invest in stocks?

Mr. D. W. D. (Dallas, Texas)

A: Absolutely not, and certainly not now. As a CPA, I think that your calculation about being ahead of the game saving on nurses and sacrificing earnings by your wife probably makes sense. But it does not so far as either your employment or your investment strategy is concerned.

Your employment strategy boils down to a bet that you will not be caught in the overhead cutbacks increasingly being forced on all big companies, and especially the profit-and-capital squeeze on oil companies. I urge you not to take tenure for granted, and to protect yourself now against the danger that you may find yourself added to the army of faithful employees separated before their pension rights vest.

Your investment strategy illustrates the high cost of CPAs doubling in brass as money managers. Endowment policies combine insurance and investment objectives, and represent inefficient ways of achieving both. You would do better to take advantage of the option your policy gives you of converting into straight life. This will yield substantial savings in annual premium costs. You need to protect yourself against the possibility of discovering that banking on your present pension rights to give you a start into retirement will prove to be pie in the sky. Bank your premium savings into the emergency reserve fund you are overdue for building.

Q: I am an electrician, age thirty-five, married, with three children. Over the past five years, my annual income has more than doubled, so that I now gross over $30,000. Naturally, I pay more taxes and have bought a second car and new furniture, as well as making larger mortgage payments on our new home. Otherwise our way of life is much the same as it was five years ago. Still, I'm no more able to put away any savings from $30,000 than when I was making $12,000. I don't believe my *problem is entirely due to the rise in cost of living. Can you give me some advice?*

Mr. J. D. (Baltimore, Maryland)

A: I agree with you that your problem is not entirely due to the rise in the cost of living. In fact, I think you are more responsible for your problem than inflation is.

The cost of the manufactured products you are buying certainly has not gone up anything like 50 percent in the last five years. True, most services have, and I imagine that your family does spend more on services than on goods. As an electrician, you are in a position to know that repair costs have been going up. This argues for you to concentrate your efforts at economy on avoiding the costs of services.

Meanwhile, the jump in your income has put you in a higher tax bracket. This means that you are in a better position to wring some savings out of another source of inflation in the cost of services, namely, property tax payments. Be sure that you claim them as a deduction on your income tax return so that you get the use of your own money instead of permitting the tax collector to have it. The same goes for your interest payments on your mortgage. Be sure that you are filing a W4 form with your withholding in order to get the benefit of all the deductions to which you're entitled each payday.

I assume that your labor contract is giving you valuable fringe benefits in the form of health insurance. If, on a $30,000 income, you can't set aside cash for emergency reserves, as well as cash for a savings reserve, I doubt that you would be able to do so on $40,000 or even $50,000.

Your problem is not financial. It is disciplinary. I suggest that you treat the cash you have been spending as a back debt involving the same kind of fixed obligation that you pay on your mortgage, and second only to it. You might tax yourself with a savings plan and bank the proceeds, keeping the change paid you as interest. You can use it.

Q: I am twelve years old, and make about $5 a week. I am thinking about buying some stock, but I really don't know too much about it. Would you please give a young investor some advice?

Mr. J. F. (Oak Park, Michigan)

A: Bully for you! You're the hope of the country. The profitable use of money, however, begins with the clear use of words. Right now, think of yourself as a saver with plans to become an investor.

Devote the next year to putting your $5 a week in a savings bank. Meanwhile, pick a stock well known in Michigan—like one of the utility companies—and keep track of its weekly price fluctuations and its quarterly dividend payments. Learn to do your planning on paper before you take your first chance doing it with real money. At the rate you're going, you'll be ready to invest while you're still a minor.

When you do, be sure that income (whether from dividends, if you buy stock; or from interest, if you buy bonds) is your main objective. Under the tax rules now in effect, the first $600 you earn, from whatever source is not taxable. This is increased by the $100 dividend extension available to all investors.

Q; I am an eighteen-year-old secretary with around $1,300 that I would like to invest. My future plans are indefinite. I don't want to tie up my money in long-term investment, but I feel this money can be invested. You have mentioned buying high-yielding bonds. Do you recommend such bonds for me?

Miss T. H. (Montpelier, Ohio)

A: You're sensible to be asking, but your question does not make sense. No one with only $1,300 is ready to start investing. All you can hope to be for some years, and many thousands of dollars more, is a saver. Anyone unwilling to tie up money for a considerable period, or not free to do so, would be better keeping money in the bank.

Q: You have repeatedly advised the "small guy" to buy as much life insurance as possible. Why? When you refer to "ordinary" life insurance, do you mean cash-value, permanent life insurance or term insurance?

Mr. R. S. (Chicago, Illinois)

A: I advise this because the small guy has almost no chance of making enough money in his lifetime to build an estate for the protection of his family anything like what he can buy by paying nominal life insurance premiums. Because the same goes for his ability to win credit standing during his lifetime, and because the cost of this protection is just about the only service to have remained inflation-free, I do mean cash-value, permanent life insurance.

Q: Why do you recommend cash-value insurance over term? I would do better buying term insurance and put-

ting the cash in the bank. Are you suggesting that many people would not bank the cash?

Mr. W. C. (*Spokane, Washington*)

A: You have not investigated the price you would pay for the "bargain" offered by term insurance over ordinary life. Even renewable term is subject to escalation in premium costs on each renewal, in line with your age at the time of renewal.

Ordinary life covers you for life at the premium cost for the age of your original purchase, without exposing you to the risk of remaining uncovered when you may no longer be able to pass a health examination. It also gives you a fringe benefit in the form of cheap loan value and an asset for credit purposes.

Term insurance is useful, but the basic service of insurance is protection. There's no substitute for ordinary life. You get what you pay for. Cutting corners for bargains runs the risk of defeating your purpose by skimping on value received.

Q: *Recently you praised a man who was carrying a $175,000 life insurance policy. I earn about the same as he does, around $23,000, but I feel that I can't afford to carry that much insurance. Why do you encourage carrying so much insurance?*

Mr. J. G. (*Lombard, Illinois*)

A: Too many people end their earning careers without having accumulated enough capital to meet their responsibilities to their beneficiaries. Some start out building a nest egg and wind up losing it. Carrying life insurance is no way to make money. All it buys is protective service. The shrewdest people who do best are most likely to have more of it.

For anyone who is going to buy insurance, the earlier in life it is bought, the more protection the insurance premium dollar will buy. The cost of future premiums for the duration of the policy is fixed in the year you bought the policy.

Q: I am a thirty-six-year-old engineer, single, earning $18,000 annually with one parent as a dependent. I have income from $50,000 in Savings and Loan accounts; $6,000 in a mutual fund; and $3,000 in Treasury notes. My only debt is $13,000 on my home, and I am able to save $9,000 a year. As I am interested either in resuming my education or going into business, my investment objective has been income, and I have considered converting some of my savings into long-term corporate bonds.

Mr. R. S. (Davenport, Iowa)

A: You are oversaving and underinsuring—even though you are not yet married. At your age, the cost of buying protection for your dependent parent is still relatively cheap. Insurance would represent a more economic use of money than oversaving.

If you do intend to start a business, remember that the number one reason for new business failure in America was underestimation of capital needs. This was true before inflation raised capital needs even higher. The possibility of your setting up in business argues against tying up your liquid availability in long-term investment. Short-term tax-free bonds would suit your purpose while you make up your mind. If you return to school, and fall into a lower tax bracket, you could then switch, without risk of loss, into higher-yielding securities.

Q: I am a forty-nine-year-old re-married widow with an estate of about $100,000. I have invested $50,000 in high-grade bonds, $12,000 in land, and have $42,000 in the bank. My second husband is a labor arbitrator, sixty-one, and in good health. He has no savings, little life insurance, and no pension. I am thinking of buying a condominium in Florida for rental income. In your column in the Chicago Tribune, *you have advised large mortgages, but wouldn't I be better off buying the property outright or having a small mortgage? I fear being saddled with a high mortgage if my husband has to retire sooner than expected.*

Mrs. S. S. (Grand Rapids, Michigan)

A: Your husband's impractical handling of his own finances is typical of the lack of realism in recent labor settlements. Tell him that responsibility—especially in anticipating marriage in middle life—begins with buying adequate life insurance. The spectacle of a labor arbitrator with no pension recalls the saying about the cobbler's son having no shoes.

In your circumstances, I wouldn't be worried about having a high mortgage—after all, the less you freeze of your capital reserve, the more you will have available for high-yielding investment to earn the interest on your mortgage. The interest you pay will be a tax deduction. Moreover, lending institutions are loaded with money and would be anxious to give anyone in your position a good deal. Tell your husband to start saving to build up a reserve against your mortgage payments.

Q: I am fifty-six years old, unmarried, and worried about my retirement income. I have $20,000 in the bank. On retirement, I will receive $175 a month in Social Security and pension. Would it be a good idea to add to my income by investing in a single payment retirement annuity which will pay me $157 a month for life?

Miss K. M. L. (Saint Clair, Pennsylvania)

A: The proposition boils down to a gamble on your life expectancy. Payments of $157 a month will give you something like $1,900 a year, which would be a very high return on a $20,000 investment. Of course, annuity payouts represent paybacks on capital and are certainly not to be considered as all income. A good way to begin arriving at a decision is to have a thorough medical examination. If your life expectancy is less than 10 years, this will not be a good deal for you. If it is greater, you will come out ahead.

Annuity computation is a complicated, specialized business for professionals, which calls for consultation between your lawyer and insurance broker. If you decide to go ahead, don't switch all of your present cash reserve into the annuity. Keep at least $2,500 in your savings account.

Q: I have read your book and recent statements on the economy in your syndicated newspaper column. My wife, a school teacher, and I have tax-deferred, variable annuity retirement programs with periodic investment in qual-

ity common stocks. You have advised holding on to cash, but have suggested that mutual funds are sound for long-term planning. We hope to work for fifteen years more. Would we be better off discontinuing our retirement programs?

Rev. J. J. (New York, N. Y.)

A: Variable annuities came into vogue back when the idea was that the stock market would keep on going up forever. Tax deferrals are more advantageous for investors in higher tax brackets. My own strong preference is for the separation of insurance and investment. Ask the salesman who sold you your program if the sponsoring company will permit you, without penalty, to split up your program into ordinary life insurance and a mutual fund. If a switch would be expensive, your fifteen-year target argues for your continuing with the program.

Q: My wife and I are fifty-eight years old, and I plan to retire at sixty-two. I am in the $10,000 income bracket, with no pension. Our home is paid for; we have no debts; and our savings amount to approximately $15,000. We recently cashed in an insurance policy, and have $19,000 to invest. Do you think government bonds would be best for us? If so, what type?

Mr. C. R. (Chicago, Illinois)

A: I think you did wrong to cash in your life insurance policy. Hanging on to it would have financed a great deal of protection. The younger you were when you bought it, the less it cost you. The older you get, now that you have dropped it, the more you will need it.

I think you will do well to continue building up your savings while buying bonds—not governments, but good corporates. Do so the moment long-term interest rates reach 8 percent. They will.

Q: I am forty, separated from my husband, and have two small children to support on my salary of $9,000. Because of the death of my uncle, I am to receive insurance amounting to $30,000. My two questions are: What kind of tax will I have to pay on the insurance? Should I take payment in one sum or in installments?

Mrs. E. P. C. (Memphis, Tennessee)

A: You need pay no tax if the insurance comes to you as a beneficiary on the death of an insured person. However, if you elect to receive your policy proceeds on an installment basis, you will earn interest on the unpaid balance due you, and this interest will be taxable.

By all means take your death benefits in one lump sum. With your two children and your low salary, you are on the spot to put the money to work earning as much extra income as possible. The faster you can have the use of the money, the better chance you will have to work out of the hole any woman in your position is bound to be in.

Q: I am a widow with a twelve-year-old daughter to support. Because of my limited education, I can only find a part-time job. This pays $140 a month so I keep my Social Security. All I have otherwise is $3,000 in a life insurance policy. My daughter is my beneficiary. Would it perhaps be better to take $2,000 out and put it in a sav-

*ings account to build money for my daughter's educa-
tion? I rent my home, and have no other assets. What can
I do to see that I have money for my daughter's future? It
is very important to me that she has all I can possibly
give her.*

Mrs. B. P. (Detroit, Michigan)

A: I respect your devotion to your daughter and grieve
for your plight. But liquidating even a penny of the insurance you have bought for her would mean jumping from
the frying pan into the fire. Your first hope is to improve
your income while practicing the strictest austerity in
your living costs. A second part-time job might be the answer.

As a working mother, your problem relates to one of
America's deepest-rooted social lacks; namely the absence
of child care centers supported by employers and communities for the benefit of parents of both sexes who want to
work, and would, to support their children—if only they
had a place they could trust to care for them during working hours. Vigilant citizenship is as much a part of your
problem as improving your income and using it economically. Write to your mayor, your congressman, and to
Chairman Wilbur Mills of the House Ways and Means
Committee (which writes your country's tax bills), explaining your need for a child care center. Chairman Mills is on
record for an investment tax credit to corporations investing in such facilities for parents whose earnings would
earn more taxes for the government.

While I am not in the employment agency business, I
know enough about the labor market, and about the concern of the various regional subsidiaries of the telephone

company for the quality of its service, to remind you that switchboard operators are in short supply. This is a prime opportunity for women needing more part-time work. Ask the Michigan Bell Telephone Company how you can qualify for its training program. If this means moonlighting, do it. The Social Security authorities have cheated the public long and systematically enough so that turnabout will be fair play until the Social Security laws are amended to recognize the need to provide incentives instead of penalties to Social Security beneficiaries willing and able to work.

Last, but not least, be frank with your daughter about your common problem. Explain to her that she needs to find a part-time job—at more than baby-sitting—even while she is still in high school. Part of every city school principal's job nowadays is to help parents like you help their youngsters of school age to help themselves. Count on your daughter's school principal to be even more sensitive to budget trouble than you are.

$
$
CHAPTER – – $ – – **6**
$
$
$ **CASH**
$
$

       One of the principal messages of *What Shall I Do With My Money?* was that the recent inflationary crisis had put an overriding premium on cash. Today cash is worth even more than it was between 1970 and 1972—for at least two reasons.

The first reflects the separate trends in the prices of goods and the cost of services. Cash is buying bargains in usable products, but paying people to do things costs more.

The second big reason why cash commands a premium is that people expect to have less cash to use. And the less they have, the more it is worth. This was true even before President Nixon's August 15 Proclamation of Emergency made it official that incomes were not going up. After August 15, the rise in both the cost of living and the cost of doing business increased the premium on cash.

Inflation is the oldest experience described in the standard texts. As everyone knows, it erodes savings relentlessly. But it also does so gradually. Stagflation, however, is a new experience. It combines the worst of both worlds —stagnation in earnings, suffered simultaneously with inflation of costs. Where past inflations have loomed as a simple threat to the buying power of cash in hand, stagflation pinches earning power as well as present buying power. It's getting as hard to make a dollar as it has been to keep it. But the harder a dollar is to make, the more every dollar earned will be worth—in spite of the higher cost of living.

The representative response of most Americans to the onset of stagflation has been prudent and realistic. Little wonder, so long as one segment of the American work force was striking for 30 percent more in green paper while another segment was getting hit with pink slips.

Certainly the worst of the stagflationary crisis has shown people demanding record pay increases the need to insure against the loss of overtime, the rise of short time, and the spread of unemployment. But they have been trusting their pay increases less than ever. Ironically, the beneficiaries of the higher cost of services have been among those running most scared of the resultant inflation. Plumbers, electricians, and other craftsmen have been earning more. But they have been spending as little as they could and saving as much as they could.

High rates of savings are not new in American economic history. The sieges of emergency controls, during World War II and the Korean War, forced surges in savings. Then, wartime controls on civilian production and wartime rationing of civilian consumption had left consumers with no alternative but to save record proportions of their record earnings. In 1971, however, consumers were free to buy anything they wanted, and every industry with goods to sell was glutted with excess capacity. Nevertheless, despite government efforts to stimulate spending, consumers hung on to their money. And, what is not necessarily the same thing, they saved more of their earnings.

1971 saw the largest increase in savings—as well as the highest rate of savings out of consumers' income—in peacetime history. The stagflationary crisis had delivered a one-two punch to consumer confidence. The old conventional wisdom had it that, in time of inflation, consumers would save less and spend more, calculating that what they purchased today would cost more tomorrow. But consumers are earners—whether their income is earned by working or unearned from investments. As living and operating costs rose, confidence fell in both earning more and keeping more.

American consumers are sensitive to losing income— more so than to dissipating it on higher costs. So long as they could count on improving their incomes, they had no hesitation in owing money. But their instinctive reaction to the combination of certainty about inflation and uncertainty about income was to clutch at cash. With less money to meet higher costs, their choice made matters worse for the economy but better for themselves. They opted for owning more cash and owing less debt.

During the last three years of crisis, the premium on cash has been measured in two different ways. In 1969 and 1970, it was measured by the unprecedentedly high rates of interest willingly paid to cash-holders by increasingly desperate borrowers. In 1971, interest rates came down—for those whose credit ratings were still good enough to get loans. The premium on cash then worked out as massive discounts available on cash purchases—from machine tools bought by business, right through to basic consumer goods. Nowhere have the benefits of being cash-rich been more apparent than in the "big-ticket" items that families buy: houses, autos, and appliances.

One of the mistakes economists make is to devise game plans as if the economy were just a money game. Instead, it is a people game played with money. One of the mistakes consumers make is to think of themselves as just buyers of goods, like groceries; or of services, like repairs. Instead, the tax-paying consumer is also buying—or being charged for—the services rendered by government. How fast one gets the use of whose money is the name of the money game. Make sure the government is not keeping your money after you have stopped owing it. If you have earned less than you expected, you are probably entitled to get some of your tax money back. And refunds are due when and as fast as your earnings fall short of estimates, not after they have.

Believe it or not, you are not the only one who is error-prone in guesstimating taxes. The tax collector pulled the biggest boner of all. A monumental underestimation of withholding rates in the 1970 form helped push the government down the road to bankruptcy in 1971. Its 1972 response was to switch to overwithholding.

The IRS, embarrassed by the successive exercises in under- and over-compensation, urged taxpayers to sharpen up their claims for refunds and, even before that, for deductions. Using the W4 form on which deductions are listed is the way to begin. By all means, do so.

Checking the sources of your income is the easiest way to determine whether or not the Treasury is banking itself on your overpayments. Hiring a tax accountant is the other way to get clear on whether you are being overwithheld each month; and on how much you will owe or, perhaps, have coming back in refunds at tax settlement time in April. Nor are you just likely to save on taxes. The fee to the tax accountant is another deduction for tax-paying consumers.

Staying even with your dollar problems means knowing how to count your net current assets. Here's how to tell if you have any.

Add up your cash on hand and in your checking account, plus savings deposits with only ninety days to go to maturity. Ninety days is the dividing line between assets and liabilities that are current and those that are long term. Do not include longer-term savings certificates, but include the interest you will be collecting on them in the next three months. Then add any other interest and dividends you will be collecting from bonds, stocks, insurance policies, or property in the next three months. Include, of course, your pay and any assets you are getting ready to sell and will get paid for within ninety days. *Don't* include the return on government savings bonds, because U.S. savings bond holders do not collect their interest on a current annual basis. Finally, add any bills owed to you.

With an accurate count of your current assets, the next step is to come to grips about what to do with your money. Getting clear about the different kinds of money, and the uses of each, is the way to do it.

"Cash" is usable spending power. To begin with, it is money—dollar bills and checking accounts. But spending power, ready to be used when and as needed, can also be held in "cash equivalents." The main categories of these are savings deposits, time deposits, Treasury bills, and commercial paper. Aggressive commercial banks offer the use of overdrafts as another cash equivalent. Overdrafts are high-cost entitlements to write checks, up to an agreed limit, without having first made a deposit. There are also credit cards, the newest form of cash equivalent.

Each type of cash equivalent has emerged in response to the needs of a particular sort of money-user. For example, where lower-income consumers keep their cash in savings deposits, big cash holdings can be put to work for short hauls in commercial paper.

When money-users keep their spending power in cash equivalents rather than in the sock under the bed, the cash they will spend tomorrow is available for someone else to spend today. Therefore, cash equivalents earn interest for their owners. The spread between interest rates on different kinds of cash and cash equivalents reflects the relative ease with which they can actually be used to make purchases in the marketplace. Dollar bills and checking accounts earn no interest—they are instantly available to the owner.

The difference between savings deposits and time deposits—sometimes known as certificates of deposit—is that time deposits tie up your money for a considerable period of time in return for a rate of interest which may seem low after it has been contracted for. As not many owners of time deposits are aware, federal regulations have put the burden on such depositors to demonstrate distress as the condition of liquidating them before maturity. Savings deposits, by contrast, pay a lower rate of return, but can be liquidated on demand without complication. Also, the interest they pay is reckoned by the day. The lower return is worth the advantage in liquidity— especially for money-users to whom income is less important than ready access to cash reserves.

During past periods of money trouble, people with

money invariably ran it out of the banks. Fear prompted them to forgo a return on their money for the sake of being sure they could hang on to it. But the unprecedented set of circumstances responsible for putting a premium on cash and, at the same time making the banks safe, has freed money-users to enjoy the best of both worlds: to stay liquid and still earn a return on liquidity.

The exception is the user of credit card "cash" who pays for the privilege like any other borrower. Credit card users operate by issuing drafts on the liquidity of the businesses selling them goods and services. Whether they know it or not, they pay a price for this privilege. The trade-off is anything from an 8 to 15 percent markup in cost for the use of the money.

Nevertheless, one argument remains for using credit cards and absorbing the price penalty built into their cost. In part, this incentive is economic. For all interest charges (including charges for the use of credit cards) are tax deductible; and all taxpayers using the long form to claim tax deductions need to keep records, which credit card users have. But part of this incentive is also noneconomic. The law-and-order crisis in America is encouraging money-owners not to carry cash. Carrying credit cards is one form of defense against the crime wave in America. Although this does not represent shrewd economic reasoning, it does represent prudent social reasoning.

Stressing the role played by devaluation of the dollar is not relevant in terms of decision-making practicalities. Devaluation is limited to just the international dollar, and means less to your pocketbook than meets the eye. People with dollars wanting to buy other currencies will pay more and get less. But, contrary to the popular talk about it, devaluation changes nothing for the domestic dollar you earn, spend, save, borrow, and invest. Hamburger won't be priced any differently because of devaluation, nor will anything else. And your dollars won't buy more or less because of devaluation. Contrary to all authoritative expectations, imports are working out as costing less —thanks to the pressure on foreign manufacturers to cut their prices to avoid being priced out of the American market. Nevertheless, for the duration of the emergency— dominated as it will be by the continuing speculation over what new controls will supersede what old controls —banking your money will be the way to hang on to it.

Not all dollars are the same, or do the same job, no matter how well off you may or may not think you are. While your cost-of-living dollar is your problem, your savings dollar is your opportunity. The experience of recent years has witnessed the pragmatic triumph of Main Street's prudence over Wall Street's sophistication. Month by month, the small investors have pulled out of the stock market. And the professional managers of big money have been left holding the bag.

The climax of the crisis, and its resolution, will find the investment dollar in your bank account worth significantly more, relative to present values, than any investment you could buy today (even though the cost-of-living dollar will no doubt be worth somewhat less). Ask anyone interested in buying a business. Cash today will buy much more in the way of assets and earning power. It will also buy more income from investments. For, if I am proven right about the stock market, it will buy you larger blocks of better stocks.

Q: I am concerned about our continuing inflation. I have a large surplus of cash in savings. At sixty-one years old, I am not interested in starting new business ventures. Isn't my money worth increasingly less? I seem to be losing more to inflation than I am making on my 5 percent savings return.

Mr. G. H. (Detroit, Michigan)

A: You are realistic in not thinking of getting involved in new business commitments. But I do not think that you are realistic in your assessment of the value of your cash investment reserve.

While some drains on the family budget—notably health costs—have been as big as 25 to 30 percent a year, the overall erosion in the cost-of-living dollar has probably not been as much as 10 percent a year. More recently, bargain pricing of goods has been helping to offset the continued inflation of the cost of services.

Meanwhile, gains in the buying power of the investment dollar have been much greater than the 5 to 10 percent losses in the cost-of-living dollar. High-quality stocks, down 75 percent from their highs, have been losing 15 percent and more a year, giving the investment dollar corresponding increases in buying power. Ask anyone still interested in buying a business if less cash won't buy better than 10 percent more in good assets and assured income than a year ago.

Why not switch some of your savings into high-rated short-term tax exempts? In spite of the recent drop in interest rates, this is an attractive investment to holders of large sums of cash, and it is loss-free.

Q: My husband and I have been married six months. We have been quarreling about our joint checking account, which my husband recently changed from a regular checking account to a charter check credit account. As I understand it, we can overdraw our account up to $1,000, but the annual compound interest on the overdraft is 12.17 percent! Since we have a savings account which we can borrow on, it seems ridiculous to pay such high interest charges. My husband says that borrowing on this checking account is a good thing because it establishes a line of credit. Which of us is right?

Mrs. R. B. C. (St. Louis, Missouri)

A: Your savings account establishes your credit. I think your family argument is confusing the purpose of a checking account—which is to pay bills—with a savings account—which is to help you get ahead of the game.

There are three kinds of checking accounts. (1) The special checking account averages a small balance. On such accounts a small sum is charged for each check written, and there is a small monthly carrying charge. (2) The regular checking account has no service charge if a minimum balance is maintained. The balance varies with the bank. It may be as low as $300 or as high as $800. (3) The charter checking account allows overdrafts up to a specified amount. Obviously, an overdraft is a loan, and banks charge interest on loans. If you need to borrow, offer to pay the going rate.

It is a form of being penny-wise and pound-foolish to get ahead of yourself building a savings account, while running short and borrowing on your checking account.

Q: Which is the safer place for savings—the banks or Savings and Loan institutions? How is it that the S & Ls can pay higher interest rates?

Mrs. A. F. (*Carmel Valley, California*)

A: All banks and Savings and Loan institutions are insured by agencies of the federal government for amounts up to $25,000. S&Ls are allowed to pay savings depositors higher interest rates than banks because the S&Ls are restricted to making nothing but mortgage loans. Therefore, they need to attract longer-term deposits. But the offset against the higher S&L rate is that S&L deposits are deemed to be savings instead of just deposits. Be sure that you are clear as to how long you must keep your money on deposit in order to qualify for the top rate of return. Terms vary from institution to institution. And be clear that the regulations applicable to time deposits in banks require depositors to prove hardship as the condition of withdrawal before their certificates mature.

Q: Last week I transferred $5,500 from our savings account paying 4½ percent to a Golden Savings Account paying 5¾ percent for two years, compounded daily. I had considered investing the money in hospital bonds which paid 8½ percent for fifteen years, but I decided to be conservative. Do you think I was right? I am sixty years old, and my wife and I have a combined income of $10,000 a year.

Mr. D. A. (*Manitowoc, Wisconsin*)

A: You are confusing investment in fifteen-year bonds with two-year savings certificates. Your problem is how to figure out where to draw the line at which your needs are satisfied and your investment programming can begin.

If this represents your savings reserve, you did right. But if your savings needs are covered, you missed out on doubling your income instead of just raising it 25 percent.

Q: We are at retirement age and expect to sell our business for cash. As individuals, how can we prevent our dollars from eroding in purchasing power? As a citizen, I'm concerned that the admitted deficit is almost exactly the amount of the interest on our $400 billion national debt. We are not only not reducing this monstrous debt, but borrowing to pay the interest. Some people see our government unable to go on borrowing. Do you agree?

Mr. V. C. B. (Spokane, Washington)

A: Your question skirts the murky borderline separating the responsible from the irresponsible. No one is more alarmed than I by the mishandling of our federal financing. The crisis is now so out of hand that whether irresponsibility or incompetence has been more to blame is rapidly becoming an academic question.

So far, so bad—and it's bad enough. Don't exaggerate it past the point of responsibility. All money will not be worthless. The federal government will be able to borrow its interest bills as they fall due because it is not a business and is not subject to the sanctions that make or break businesses. Ironically, the overextended position of the Federal Treasury reinforces its ability to make good its commitment to insure bank deposits: its borrowings become acceptable, usable money as fast as it circulates them. Meanwhile, as a practical matter, the more the

Treasury has to borrow to pay its interest, the higher it will push interest rates and, therefore, the less its outstanding debt placed at lower interest rates will be worth. This is one good reason why prudent investors are avoiding any U.S. Treasury debt not shortdated.

As to your private question, worry about how many dollars in cash you will have to fortify yourselves with, not how little each dollar will be worth to you. Take advantage of the inflationary spiral of interest rates to get a higher rate of return for not working than your business has been able to net you for working.

Q: Please explain what a U. S. Treasury bill is. Is it risky? Or is it covered by some form of U. S. insurance? Would you recommend it as an investment?

Miss C. V. (Denver, Colorado)

A: A Treasury bill is a short-term debt instrument, ranging up to one year; but most bills are issued with maturities of 90 or 180 days; 9-month and 12-month bills are also available. The Treasury sells its bills as often and as fast as it needs money. Treasury bills are not investment securities. They are interest-bearing cash equivalents.

It would be pointless for the Treasury to insure its own debt because it would have to issue the paper to make good its own default. As a practical matter, all Treasury paper is "money-good." The investor can count on getting his interest and the face amount of the bill promptly at maturity. If he needs his money before the bill comes due, he can sell it for cash without any loss of interest, which is prorated on a daily basis.

Although Treasury bills are fashionable with a host of

amateur savers, they are not a medium for either savings or investment. They represent a way of holding cash at short term, and getting paid for it. When interest rates are high, Treasury bills pay a higher rate of return than savings accounts. Ironically, the people who trust stocks and bonds less wind up trusting Treasury bills more. Moreover, the way this topsy-turvy money world of ours works, they are right.

Q: I am a widow, age seventy-eight, and in fine health. I have $50,000 in certificates of deposit and will soon receive $10,000 from the sale of my house. I'm afraid of brokers, but I wonder if I don't have too much money invested in certificates of deposit?

Mrs. L. G. (Pompano Beach, Florida)

A: Your problem is that you have confused cash with investment. It makes no sense for any individual in your circumstances to freeze so much money in certificates of deposit, which are useful either as a way to hold cash reserves or to save up investment availability.

Certificates of deposit are cash equivalents, although not as readily usable as demand deposits in checking accounts. They also tie up larger sums than are insured by banks in savings accounts. Like deposits in savings accounts, certificates of deposit are time deposits—that is, they pay interest at a fixed rate over a stipulated number of months. Interest rates on certificates of deposit do *not* fluctuate with money market conditions as Treasury bills do. They are mainly for businesses and businessmen needing to negotiate bank loans and under pressure, literally, to "buy" credit from banks by putting up deposits.

I can understand your not trusting brokers to pick stocks for you. But it is almost impossible for them to go wrong in the selection of "good name" bonds which will earn you a much higher return than certificates of deposit. The first trick is to prevent brokers from talking you into buying stocks for higher commissions. The second trick is to prevent brokers willing to accept the lower commission on bonds from buying them for you when they yield less than 8 percent.

Q: I am a thirty-four-year-old bachelor who earns $8,600 as a draftsman. I have $5,500 in savings, 200 shares in a convertible fund, 130 shares of a convertible stock, 40 shares in a utility, and one $5,000 utility bond. I am able to save $4,000 a year, including dividends from my investments. Do I sell any part of my holdings, or would I be better off sitting tight until the economy gets out of trouble?

Mr. T. R. (Cincinnati, Ohio)

A: To my mind, the way to sit tight is to sell your holdings. I think you'll do better sitting in cash, as I expect cash to build more buying power in stocks than I trust stocks to build their convertibility into cash.

Q: My husband and I are in business together, and we make about $4,000 a month. We have four children and about $9,000 in savings. We know nothing about stocks but are interested in investing around $25,000. We follow your syndicated newspaper column and want to know what you would suggest.

Mrs. C. M. (Pacific Grove, California)

A: Could you increase your earnings from your business by investing more of your reserve in it? The business you know about is doing pretty well. Could it do better?

It's getting too hard to stay ahead of the game to tie up your liquid reserve investing in a game you don't know how to play. Keep it in a savings account. Family businesses go under by underestimating their money needs. In any case, the increasingly erratic behavior of the stock market suggests that time has been running out on the happy days when investment amateurs could count on making money in the stock market.

Q: The wage-price ceiling seems to indicate a weakness rather than a solution. I have little confidence in the administration and I expect a further dollar devaluation, a depression, or a more severe inflation when the present controls are removed. What do you think of foreign silver and gold stocks, silver and gold bullion, silver coins and Swiss franc bank accounts for the small investor?

Mr. W. D. (Chicago, Illinois)

A: I entirely agree with your suspicions, but not with your conclusions. Cash, the domestic American dollar, remains any investor's best friend.

I agree with you about the prudence of running scared. I do not agree with you that the turbulence in the foreign exchange markets will hurt the buying power of the domestic dollar. Silver has been frustrating more speculators than the stock market; Canadian and American gold stocks have been anticipating stabilization of the price of gold at a higher level than seems likely; while the South African gold stocks refuse to perform like moneymakers even when the news is pointing to a "once-in-a-generation" opportunity offered by them. Silver bullion is a speculative will-o'-the-wisp. And the Swiss no longer pay interest on "hot money" from abroad. Count your blessings and keep your cash in your neighborhood bank.

Q: Now that Japan has revalued her currency, does the wise investor buy a future in Japanese yen on the money market?

Mr. G. G. (Danville, Illinois)

A: The shrewd speculator knows enough to avoid this trap. All Japanese markets are regulated against foreigners. The plug is pulled out from under them whenever each new wave of foreign speculation brings a rush of Western currency in.

Q: I am considering depositing $15,000 in a national bank in Mexico, paying 13.3 percent. Do you think this would be safe? As to the interest, would I have to pay federal tax if I collect it here or there?

Mrs. E. S. (Cassopolis, Michigan)

A: High rate deposits in Mexican banks have been safe and popular until now. But the international monetary muddle is hurting Mexico and she has loaded herself with very burdensome foreign interest charges. Moreover, the Mexican peso is tied to the dollar; and, because Mexico owes a good deal of foreign debt in European currencies which have been marked up, the cost of servicing her debt is now even more burdensome than it was. Think of this 13.3 percent rate as a flashing red light for risk, not a green light for greed. As a practical matter, I think that you will find that the rates offered by reputable Mexican banks have dropped closer to 9 percent.

If you know what is good for you, you had better pay the federal tax on any such income.

Q: I read your syndicated newspaper column regularly and have been following your seemingly out-of-step view that the foreign currencies which have been the big winner against the dollar are now vulnerable and are about to lose their gains. I am beginning to find confirmation of your forecast in the form of short-selling by international speculators of the German Deutschemark. The renewed speculation in the European gold market is also providing it. Do you think the present international monetary crisis is now reaching a climax where it will pay to play the gold market?

Mr. J. R. (New York, N. Y.)

A: I certainly think the international monetary crisis is nowhere near being resolved. No doubt a second dollar crisis will flare up before the traveling storm hits the currencies of the dollar-holding countries which have been regarded as strong. As it does, devaluation will loom as a real possibility for the Deutschemark and other recently revalued currencies. The jump in the so-called free gold market is a portent of this, although I do not see the price of gold fulfilling the die-hard goldbug projections of a new gold market stabilization at $75–100 an ounce.

You'll do well to recall that the official $35 gold peg committed the U. S. Treasury to take all gold offered at that price, while the $38 price merely represents a token level at which the U. S. Treasury will neither buy nor sell gold. I do not expect any new undertaking by the U. S. Treasury to support the gold market at some inflated price—not least because this would invite everyone who bought gold from the U. S. Treasury at $35 to dump it back at the inflated price.

Under the Gold Reserve Act of 1934, no U. S. citizen may legally own gold. I see little chance of the present legal prohibition being modified in any way, and I see every indication that the federal government will continue enforcing it rigidly. Thinking of ways to make money begins with knowing what temptations to avoid because they are legally out of bounds.

Q: I am sixteen years old and have $2,000 in the bank earning 5¾ percent interest. Right now the money is under my father's control, and he thinks a bank is the best place for it because the amount is too small for investment. But after seeing an editorial on television advising people to invest in diamonds, I am wondering if that would be a better way to use my money.

Mr. J. K. (Chicago, Illinois)

A: Believe it or not, the old man is making sense. Diamonds and other non-income-bearing assets are good inflation hedges, but only for people rich enough to be able to invest on a large scale and to employ expert management to select the particular items with particular assets most likely to command a premium. $2,000 cannot begin to do this. But some banks are now paying 6 percent or more on savings, which in twelve years would double your money—so long as you don't touch it in that time.

By then you will be earning enough on your own to make direct investment in assets worth your while.

Q: My seventy-nine-year-old mother owns around 170 acres of farmland which she can sell at $400 an acre. After selling, her only income—over and above a monthly Social Security check of $75—will be what she can get on the $68,000 the sale of her land would bring her. What would be the most advisable way to invest to provide for her living expense and to avoid capital gain tax?

Mrs. S. D. (La Porte, Indiana)

A: Your mother would do well to keep at least one-fourth of her capital in savings accounts to provide for any medical emergencies or running health costs. At her age, and with the liquidity she will have, I see no reason for her not to live on some capital. After all, that's what it's for. If the balance is invested in good bonds, the yield will be pretty close to 8 percent. This would seem adequate to cover her needs. Be sure that you remember to find out how much capital gain tax she will owe.

Q: I know the puritan virtues are out of fashion now. But I still don't like the notion of going into debt. Since borrowing money seems to be the only way of establishing credit, can you explain to me why—if I have the cash —credit is so important?

Mr. A. L. (Portland, Maine)

A: Time was when having money to use meant having cash. Today, times are different. People with cash can and do find it cheaper to rent it out while using credit for certain needs. As the present crisis deepens, this apparent paradox will grow less paradoxical and more apparent.

Moreover, credit is often more convenient and safer to use than cash. And safety is an important consideration for older people who tend to have more cash and are less able to protect themselves. Especially with today's alarming rise in crimes—which are no longer restricted to large urban areas—anybody walking around with large sums of cash is a likely candidate for a blow on the head and an empty pocket. If such an unpleasant event did occur, and the victim needed hospital care, unfortunately it would be necessary for him to prove his ability to pay. On weekends, when banks aren't open, a millionaire who can't prove he is good for $10 is just another vagrant. A credit card is a money-good passport to guaranteeing entitlement to emergency services. Credit is not only as good as —but very often better than—cash. You can never know how much cash you may need in time of emergency. Proving instant credit availability eliminates the problem.

As to your opinion of borrowing, if inflation continues to speed up, anyone interested enough in the old-fashioned puritan virtues can make more money borrowing than working. The recipe for doing so is to pay back dollars borrowed today with dollars worth less tomorrow. Anyone with cash can be sure of playing this game without running the familiar borrowers' risk of becoming overextended or incurring short-term liabilities. No one with an assured income can lose borrowing at long-term subject to rates of interest covered by income.

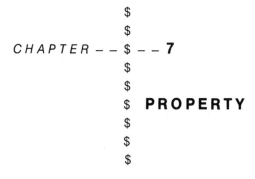

CHAPTER – – $ – – 7

$ **PROPERTY**

The boom-and-bust swings of the old-era business cycle caused more violent fluctuations in property values and real estate prices than even in the stock market. The speculative exuberance inspired by such violent upswings is built into the game of piggyback, technically known as leverage, which property owners are invited to play by investing a minimum of their own money and borrowing a maximum of mortgage money.

The financial distress spread by the corresponding violence of "shakeout" downswings is invited by the inherently illiquid nature of all property and real estate investment—by contrast with securities, which are readily salable, at relatively small day-to-day discounts during periods of market distress, and with only nominal sums needed to "make a market" and establish a current market price and a continuous market price trend. This is reason enough for a special warning against exposure to the common entrapment of committing to buy a new home, or actually buying it before having the money in hand from the sale of the old house.

A basic paradox confronts the money-user eying property investment. In terms of the characteristics of the property market, no investment medium is more speculative. But in terms of the needs and aims of all money-users—amateur and professional alike, family-sized and corporate—no use of money qualifies more genuinely for bona fide investment status. In terms of investment results, moreover, no use of money is likely to prove more satisfactory year in and year out—that is, provided that the financing basis on which it is bought and held makes conservative allowance for the inherently suspect character of speculative bubbles as well as for the inherently dangerous character of illiquidity panics.

Buying a home is the first and most important investment any family can make. Admittedly, in a certain number of big cities, renting has been at least temporarily more convenient than home owning. But realistic investing begins with property investment. One good reason for this reflects the difference between a concentration of the use of money and scatteration. Concentration is economic; and the momentous step involved in buying a home has a sobering effect on sober families. Amateur dabbling in the stock market, however, invites the scatteration of resources by precisely the people who can least afford to lose a little here or there and to wind up without having used all of it to advance a family purpose and to meet a basic family need.

Home owning is a more economic way of living than renting. The U.S. tax code institutionalizes this fact of financial life, for it encourages home owning by qualifying two basic costs of home owning as federal tax deductions. The first is all interest on mortgage payments. The second is all property taxes. This favored treatment to homeowners contrasts with other costs necessary to earning a living. Significantly, public transit and car maintenance for getting back and forth to work are not deductions.

While the tax code favors homeowners, it leaves tenants in an exposed condition. For whether they know it or not, the cost of their landlords' interest on mortgage debt and property taxes is passed on to them. Rent control regulations, in fact, have increasingly granted explicit permission to landlords to cost-plus their property tax increases in pass-throughs to their tenants. At the landlord level, these increases (mortgage borrowing during the recent credit crunch has provided for interest rate escalation, too) are deductible. At the tenant level, they are not. But, vital though tax considerations are, they are not decisive. In the case of the advantages offered by home owning, the tax incentive reinforces the economic soundness of going this route to capital accumulation.

Looking back over the forty-year span since the last depression, more people have made more money buying homes for their own use—with no thought to profit, much less with any speculative angle at the time—than any other way: certainly more than in the stock market. Moreover, the people who have ended up making money through home owning have taken the second hurdle involved in making money—they have hung on to it. They have had something tangible to show for it and to pass along to their families, in the form of bigger and better homes bought with the profits made selling their original homes. The tax code is consistent in giving homeowners who make a profit selling their homes an advantage not enjoyed by any other tax-paying profit takers in America. This incentive frees them from the obligation to pay any capital gain tax provided they re-invest the entire pro-

ceeds of the sale, or more, into their new home within
one year.

Home buying does not grant immunity from the stern
sanction of the rule limiting rent costs to 25 percent of
the family budget. Computation of rent by the homeowner is more complicated and involves considerable
record-keeping—as, indeed, all prudent money-using
does. "Rent" for the homeowner begins with the cost of
interest plus mortgage debt payback (amortization is the
term). Owning a home outright merely cancels this basic
cost of rent. The same basic computation is not avoided.
Instead, it involves figuring how much the cash tied up in
the home could have been earning, net of taxes, instead
of using borrowed money with the deductible interest
feature.

The other components of the homeowner's rent calculation include taxes, insurance, and maintenance. One
sound way for a young family to grow up into a home
large enough to serve its future needs, but too large for it
to afford at the time of purchase, is to buy a multi-dwell-
ing home and rent out the space it is not ready to afford.

Just as a backward look over the generation of prosperity since the last depression shows how widely profitable
a well-financed housing boom can be, so the housing
boom of 1970–72 warns how risky it can be. The calculation of rent for the homeowner in terms of the 25 percent
cost-of-living rule reveals the difference. Back when the
housing boom was sound enough for its strength to be
self-propelling, homes cost less. So did the inescapable
"parasite" fees—like moving, title insurance, and legal
fees at closing, and the familiar repair jobs that greet all
new occupants of their own homes.

On the investment side of the ledger, down payments make the difference. The greater the down payment, the lower the carrying charges. Moreover, back when home-owners were making down payments—and minimizing carrying charges which were lower—they were also im-proving their cost-income ratios through overtime, pro-motions, and pay increases.

The contrast with the 1970–72 building boom could not be more complete. It has been concentrated in popu-lar-price housing whose cost, however, has been inflated to the $20,000–25,000 bracket. Down payments have become the exception and not the rule. Such cash as the buyers have had has tended to be dissipated in closing and moving costs. Worse still, their no-down-payment commitments to uneconomically high carrying charges have coincided with the universal absence of overtime and with the spread of short time and with unemploy-ment.

The combination of flimsy finance on the part of the builders and the high cost of building lower-grade homes has forced the choice of sites where land costs are rela-tively low. The result has been to increase commuting costs for those members of the work force least able to af-ford it. They are also the ones who take the biggest chances when robbing their rent budgets to pay for the high cost of running their cars or for more expensive transit fares.

Where the great building boom of the mid-century years qualified as well financed, the building boom of 1970–72 is suspect because it succumbed to the tempta-tion of flimsy finance which, when abused, is responsible for the speculative instability of unsound real estate practice. The fact that the government invited and underwrote it does not minimize the danger but accentuates it. Builders will always build when the cost is "on the house" —as it always is when the lending institutions are bulging with money. When builders can borrow more than they spend—"financing out" is the term—without recourse to their own credit, they build until either they run out of no-down-payment customers or their no-down-payment customers run out of payment money.

The fact that the flimsy finance responsible for the 1970–72 boom resulted in a foreclosure wave is prejudicial only to unsoundly financed and unsoundly built property, not to property investment as such. One extenuating circumstance is insurance against the buildup of credit difficulties as the aftermath to the 1970–72 building boom. It is implicit in the fact that the home buyers involved in delinquencies and foreclosures will not be losing their savings. Instead, they will become renters elsewhere until the next time incomes build up enough to support a return to down-payment home financing.

Mortgaging is the economically sound and profitable way to own property. But this does not mean that owing money with no equity to back up the debt is sound. Overborrowing on property is as uneconomic as refusing to owe anything at all on it. The test of overborrowing for families is two-fold: (1) whether the cost of carrying their debt comes to more than 25 percent of their cost of living; and (2) whether their debt is more than two-thirds the price they could get by selling their home. A home that could be sold for $50,000 is clearly overborrowed if a $45,000 mortgage is owed on it. By the same token, the same home is not overborrowed if only $30,000 is owed on it—that is, provided the cost of carrying the $30,000 debt does not exceed 25 percent of the owner's net after-tax income, before provision for insurance and savings. In the case of the business, professional, and commercial property investor, the test of overborrowing is simpler: whether the cost of carrying debt is greater than the income it earns.

Land is a law unto itself—and not merely so far as property investment is concerned. The basic difference between land and any and all other assets is that the government cannot print it. The supply is fixed independently of what government may do to create more, as it does with the money supply. The government may be responsible for, or indulge, the destruction of land, but its inflationary bias cannot overcome the fixed limits of the land supply. Waves of speculation may cause temporary fits of indigestion—they have and they will. But while the values of improved property fluctuate and go through cycles of renovation and replacement, and while the value of money depreciates over any considerable time span, the value of land always appreciates.

The present movement of money into land is a knee-jerk reaction to spiraling labor costs and reflects a shrinkage of confidence in other forms of investment. For land is the investment alternative that offers the surest way to make money while an inflationary squeeze is on. Granted, property taxes on land rise during periods of inflation, but land values rise at a much greater rate. With labor contracts up for renegotiation next year, the prospect is for an even bigger land rush.

As with all investment calculations, however, a trade-off is involved in property investment. It involves time.

While time is running in favor of landowners, they are forced to forgo income and to defer profit. And since the profit built into land is long-term, prudent landowners need other sources of unearned income to average out their overall return and offset the income sacrificed by land investment. They also need to cover the cash cost of paying taxes on land while waiting for future demand to enhance its value.

Land taxes are more than an incidental consideration, since tax collectors all over the country are under pressure to tap new sources of revenue. Meanwhile, landowners are, so to speak, banking future land profits by holding and accumulating unused land earning no present income. The incentive of the owners of unused land is to avoid accruing income taxes in the present, and to play for capital appreciation in the future. This minimizes their immediate exposure to the tax assessor (unused land invites immeasurably lower tax assessments than used land). The countervailing pressure on the tax assessor is to step up anticipatory tax assessments on landowners.

If investment programming begins with property investment in the form of home buying, it by no means ends there. After buying a home—and before dabbling in securities—the second investment step for the prudent investor to take is to buy a piece of land as a speculation on the future. The calculation on which to buy land is twofold: first, that no basic living costs will be reduced, deferred, or recaptured; and, second, that no income will be realized in this tie-up of cash. Where home buying represents an alternative to paying rent, land buying assumes an availability of free investment cash. It scarcely needs be added that no prudent investor ever

finances such tie-up of cash either by tapping savings reserves or confusing a speculative cash set-aside in a piece
of land with the 25 percent rule governing the cost of
rent. The ratio of speculative set-asides in whatever form
—securities, commodities, property or land—limits it to 10
percent of net investment assets after debt.

I recall as a young man, at the end of the last depression, being told by the first client I had as an economic
consultant, the late James Quigg Newton of Denver (one
of the shrewdest as well as most socially-minded finan-
ciers I have ever known) that big money is made not continuously but in big moves. He said that the biggest
money young investors starting up on their own could
ever hope to make for themselves was to be made by putting a small amount of money into a piece of land neither
too close to where anyone was living at the time nor that
far away. It was the most profitable advice in which I
have ever shared, either as receiver or giver.

As America has grown older, it has begun to repeat the
experience of older countries—notably in the case of land
investment. American landowners have increasingly
adopted the policy of the churches and the great noble
families of Europe. They prefer never to sell land but always to accept payment in the form of ground rents from
users anxious, willing, and able to finance putting it to
use. As this policy has spread, so has the realization that
property investment is too cumbersome and intricate to
be handled on a do-it-yourself basis.

Sociologically speaking, most people who deal in real
property do not understand securities and are better off
not trying. The same goes for professional dealers in securities. The dependence of the nonprofessional property

investor on professional management is part and parcel of the real estate business. Nonprofessional investors in securities have been learning the same lesson. Of course, the principle by no means guarantees that all candidates who claim to qualify as professional management will pass muster.

Selectivity of professional management presents as serious a problem for the property investor as for the amateur investor in securities. Consistency of past performance is no guarantee of good management. Diversification is the practical way to insure it. Reliance upon competition between professional managements—of property as well as of securities—is the amateur investor's best defense. If this strategy is good enough for General Motors in the management of its pension funds, it is good enough for the amateur investor substantial enough to take advantage of the incentives of hiring professional property management.

The advantages of property investment have led to the formation of many real estate investment trusts. They can be classified in four general categories: both short-term and long-term mortgage trusts, equity trusts, and those that represent a combination of all three types. A great deal of public money has gone into these vehicles for property investments, but I think that the efforts made so far to use REITs as the vehicle to bridge the gap between property investment and securities investment are less than satisfactory.

As so often happens with innovative investment movements, an idea whose time has come is apt to be rushed into practice with too much too soon. Rethinking is in order for the premises on which the REIT movement has been structured. Four general criticisms have been provoked against the four classes of REITs which have evolved. Each of these criticisms is more or less applicable to all of them.

The first follows from the option open to REITs to pass the tax shelter they enjoy on to their investors. Registered mutual investment companies enjoy the privilege of paying out 90 percent of their income as dividends which are taxable only to their shareholders. And because the regulations applicable to REITs have been modeled in good part from those applicable to mutual funds, this privilege has been extended to REITs as well. But real estate investment trusts are by definition different from mutual investment funds. Real estate investment requires the concentration of relatively large sums in relatively few investment properties. REITs are, therefore, not free to diversify their investment capability over a wide portfolio of holdings, none of them large enough to carry the perquisites of control or the risks of failure. Registered investment companies are not free to do anything else (see Chapter 8, "Mutual Funds").

The marketability of portfolio securities is meant to protect mutual funds against illiquidity. (The emergency provision granting them the right to make pro rata distributions of their securities during a liquidity or market crisis is a feasible supporting alternative.) But illiquidity and unmarketability are a built-in danger in all real estate investment. REITs, in competing for popular and, therefore, unsophisticated investor acceptance by paying out 90 percent of their incomes, lose the protection against the twin dangers of illiquidity and unmarketability which only a strong cash reserve position built up with retained earnings can guarantee.

The second criticism invited by the REIT concept in its present form is due to the restriction paralleling that applicable to mutual funds against their controlling the assets in which they invest. To be sure, like mutual funds, REITs have management affiliates, which may and do enjoy the perquisites of control. But investors in the securities of REITs own equities in real estate companies which may own property but not manage it.

The third criticism follows from the special-purpose nature of the three specialty classes of REITs. In the case of equity trusts, assets are concentrated in a few large investments. This exposes their investors to the dangers of substantial loss if one of their properties goes bad. This is always a possibility—especially for new investment vehicles formed at the crest of an era of confidence and, therefore, of high market capitalizations of future earnings expectations that are greater than past income collections. Such high points for confidence generally coincide with peaks for the construction cycle and are followed by erratic swings, from tight mortgage market conditions in which no leveraging is feasible to easy mortgage market conditions in which over-leveraging is a temptation.

In the case of long-term mortgage trusts, investors might just as well be buying bonds. Investors in short-term mortgage REITs are exposed to a twin hazard. The first is that their managements may underestimate the vulnerability of their building business borrowers to building cost inflation. They may, therefore, wind up owning uncompleted construction. The second is that their managements may overestimate the ability of building business operators, who are habitually short of cash and anxious to borrow whatever they can, to carry high-cost debt burdens in a period of over-indebtedness. Second, or wraparound, mortgages are particularly risky, and recall the troubles responsible for the financial distress that developed before the 1929 crash and was subsequently aggravated by it.

A fourth difficulty hampering the real estate investment trust movement has unavoidably followed the circumstances of their launching. The temptation to get liquid by unloading illiquid assets on a public impressed with "big-name" magic, at prices which involve optimistic projections for income flows and property values, is obvious.

The turbulence which the real estate investment trust stocks began to encounter in 1971 and 1972 confirms these four fears. It recalls and resembles the disappointments suffered by performance mutual funds which raised large sums from the public and felt obliged to commit them just when the stock market was nearing one of its erratic peaks of recent years. Many REIT managements have been in a similar rush to get fully invested in an overpriced market as if the popularity of a new securities-selling idea necessarily coincides with the prudence of a property-buying opportunity. The mutual fund idea has survived the timing miscalculations of performance funds; and no doubt the real estate investment trust movement will survive any troubles brought on by its "knee-jerk" compulsion to buy property from private operators as fast as it found itself selling securities to the public.

In *What Shall I Do With My Money?* I rendered two anticipatory judgments about the future popularization of property investment. The first, unfavorable, was related to the real estate investment trusts. The second, favorable, anticipated the Americanization of the new British medium of the property mutual fund which, by contrast with

REITs, is a special-purpose medium designed for investment in property as property, and not as an alternative to securities. In this respect, as in so many others, America is in the position of looking to Britain as the new frontier of investment practice: witness the mutual fund itself. Property mutual funds are Britain's latest form of institutional investment pioneering—some of London's leading merchant banking firms have already presided over such pioneering. This medium, however, still remains "futures" for America. And I regard property mutual funds as the coming thing.

Nevertheless, the merchandising apparatus of the mutual fund industry is both flexible and resourceful. The demand for professional property investment from people accustomed and able to invest in securities, but having no comparable orientation toward property investment, will eventually find an outlet improvised for it by American fund sponsors. The hard times coming for the securities markets will encourage fund managers to diversify into the management of proper property funds.

Q: We are in our late forties with a gross income of $16,000. Our home is clear, but we are thinking of borrowing $12,000 at 7 percent. You have always advocated carrying a mortgage. Do you think interest rates will come down? We are a little hesitant to commit ourselves with all the talk about devaluation.

Mr. S. A. (Chicago, Illinois)

A: You are confusing the devaluation of the international dollar with the inflation of the domestic dollar. Inflation benefits the debtor who is able to pay off in dollars that will be worth less. Inflation, therefore, argues for home owning subject to mortgage borrowing.

I do expect interest rates on home mortgages to come down some more, but not much. I believe that they are getting low enough to represent bargains for homeowners in this inflationary period. The next big surprise in the mortgage market will come when the lending institutions pull back on making new loan commitments to dubious creditors, even though they are bulging with cash they are anxious to put to work. A credit standing will determine the availability and the cost of mortgage money from here on out even more than in the past.

Q: My folks are in their late sixties and will retire in June. They plan to sell their $20,000 home and move to Florida. A salesman there told them they could get a $15,000 mortgage, even at their age. But wouldn't it be a better idea for them to pay cash?

Mr. F. A. (Durham, North Carolina)

A: Age is not a qualification for making a mortgage loan. The lending institutions go by appraised value, plus the ability of the borrower to service the loan and pay it back.

Contrary to the implication of your question, older people are on notice to think of what the surviving mate can hope to realize when the time comes to sell. Mortgage-lending is a criterion of market value for an asset that is inherently illiquid. It follows that the higher the mortgage a lending institution will make, the greater the market value a homeowner can reasonably expect to realize on resale.

Q: I am a thirty-two-year-old bachelor with no invest-
ments. My gross income is $18,000, with a good deal
going to Uncle Sam. I am thinking of buying a home in
the $34,000 bracket. One concern is the high interest
rates of over 7 percent. I could afford a down payment of
one-fourth of the purchase price. How practical is such an
investment for a single man? As my credit rating is lim-
ited to time payments on two cars, would a mortgage be
difficult to secure?

Mr. M. N. (Skokie, Illinois)

A: The more your taxes cost you, the less interest on a
mortgage will cost you—after all, it is deductible. An interest rate under 8 percent can no longer be considered
high on a $34,000 home. Before getting involved in meet-
ing your mortgage payments, however, you would do
well to take a hard look at the installments you owe on
your two cars. Why not consider getting rid of one car
and owning the other outright, even if it means making a
slightly smaller down payment on the future house?
Home ownership is the best investment you can make,
and it would give you valuable tax deductions.

You'll have no trouble getting a mortgage for 75 percent of your purchase price, so long as you can convince
your bank that you can keep abreast of your payments.
Just remember that when some smart girl lands you, she
may not like the house.

Q: My wife and I are in good health, are adequately
insured, and hope to retire in fifteen years with an in-
come of around $15,000. My salary is $13,000; savings are
$10,000; home valued at $17,000; no debts; and over

$10,000 in mutual funds. We own and manage multiple rental units and plan to buy more property. Is real estate a good method for creating retirement income? In buying real estate, is it better to put a lot or a little down?

Mr. I. E. (Fort Lauderdale, Florida)

A: "If you know what you are doing," is the answer to the first question. But your second question indicates that you may not have the necessary expertise. The profitable way to buy real estate is to put down as small a payment as possible and to get as big and as long-term a mortgage as you can.

Q: In buying a home, you have advised low down payments and long mortgages. Why is it wise to pay off a mortgage over a long period of time with interest rates so high today?

Mr. D. R. (Moscow, Idaho)

A: The tax code explains my reasoning. I assume that all mortgage borrowers need income with which to make their payments; and that they owe taxes on their income. But amortization payments are not tax deductible. By contrast, dollars paid in interest are tax deductible and, therefore, less expensive to pay with a mortgage-lender's money. As a matter of fact, mortgage interest rates are lower than they were, and seem likely to drop still lower for solid home buyers willing and able to put substantial equities behind their borrowings. Three reasons explain why mortgage lenders will intensify their search for money-good borrowers on good properties. The first is the rise in savings. The second is the rise in credit delinquencies on residential mortgages owed by borrowers with little or no equity who are unable or unwilling to meet their payments. The third is the drop in demand for commercial mortgage money.

Q: I am a forty-eight-year-old single woman earning $17,600 a year. My cash position is $23,000 with 41 shares of IBM; $1,500 in company stock; $2,000 in municipal bonds; and $7,000 savings in my employee stock purchase plan. I have no pension rights as I recently left a job. If I do not remain with my present employer, I am considering giving up my high-rise apartment—renting at $280 a month—and buying a small house. I expect this would provide a tax shelter. Do you suggest a home purchase in view of my circumstances?

Miss E. R. (Chicago, Illinois)

A: Yes, and this is a good time for cash buyers like yourself to pick up values at a bargain. Your money will do more for you in the next couple of years in your own home than in even the best stocks. Employee purchase plans compound the risks of employment and the risks of investment—as if either weren't risky enough by itself. I think you would be better off switching your employee stock investment into your home purchase, too.

As to the tax shelter you would get from owning and living in a single-occupancy home, it would be limited to mortgage interest and property taxes. In order to get an additional deduction for depreciation, you would have to buy a home big enough to produce rental income.

Q: We still owe $15,000 on our home mortgage, which was originally $25,000. Our interest rate is 5 percent.

Now, our Savings and Loan association is offering to reset the entire mortgage at $30,000 if we will accept a 7¾ percent interest rate. In your newspaper column, you have advised homeowners to get the biggest mortgage possible, as we did. But we are now worried about taking on new debt and higher carrying charges. I am a salesman, and my earnings have been dropping.

Mr. W. M. (Garden City, New York)

A: You are absolutely right to be worried about accepting this offer. I wish that Savings and Loan associations were less anxious to put mortgage money to work and more worried about overloading the customers with debt.

Nevertheless, mortgage borrowing is the most economic way to own a home. Moreover, I think the anxiety of the Savings and Loan associations is creating a borrowing opportunity for prudent money-users. But I have always conditioned this policy recommendation with a warning not to let rent or mortgage carrying charges come to more than 25 percent of net after-tax income. The fact that your income is caught up in the earnings deflation, at a time when all good property is being caught up in the tax inflation, does argue for you to take a hard new look at your borrowing limit.

Q: I am fifty-seven, and will be retiring in eight years. At present my wife and I rent a quiet duplex for $100 a month. Would I be further ahead by continuing as is, or putting $1,000 down on buying a house which we would plan to sell when I retire?

Mr. L. F. S. (Detroit, Michigan)

A: Sounds to me like your rent is a real bargain, because rents are headed up. The fiasco of Phase Two has not been suspending this pressure on the marketplace. Moreover, tenants in good properties wanting service know that its cost is rising; and that the alternative to paying for it will be going without.

Although home ownership becomes a more expensive proposition when building costs and interest rates rise, rents for most tenants have been literally going through the roof, so that home ownership is still relatively more attractive. You, however, are ahead of the landlord-tenant game; if you can stay ahead, do so. What's more, you can't buy much of a house nowadays with $1,000 down.

Q: I am a widow aged fifty-five and I have been reading your books and your newspaper column for many years. I have followed the advice in your column and was fortunate in selling out my substantial stock market position in time to protect my capital against this last year of stock market speculation.

I have no earning power, but I do need income. For some months, I have been considering a proposition to invest units of $25,000, each yielding 7 percent in tax-free income, in a number of apartment house syndications across the country. President Nixon's emergency freeze on rents last August made this proposition seem less attractive to me—especially because he did not freeze property taxes at the same time. Inasmuch as you have been emphasizing that property values are the principal beneficiaries from inflation—and you regard income from bonds as too low and the stock market still too risky—do

you think that the rent situation is working out to the ad-
vantage and security of investors in this kind of project?

Mrs. R. D. (Atlanta, Georgia)

A: I do not. The game between rent control and rent escalation is becoming a bigger football game than the Rose Bowl—and it's all thorns.

What you would be buying with this proposition is not property but a raffle ticket on the competence and the integrity of the managements offering it. I can't put enough emphasis on this condition to which property investment is subject: that while it does indeed offer the best vehicle for riding out inflationary storms, it works out well only to the extent that the property management managing the money invested makes it work out well.

The one exception to this rule is investment in raw land, which requires no management; but it also yields no income and, therefore, is a luxury reserved for the patient rich.

Q: I paid $10,000 for my home, but now believe it
could be worth as much as $25,000. My wife and I are
both in our late fifties and we have been talking about
moving to a smaller place in the country now that our
children have grown up and left home. Will I have to pay
capital gains tax on any profit I make on selling our pres-
ent home?

Mr. S. T. B. (Los Angeles, California)

A: If you buy yourself a new house and start living in it within a year, either before or after the sale, you avoid paying tax on all the proceeds so long as your new home costs at least as much as the price you receive for the old one. But if it costs *less*, you are liable to pay tax on the difference. The same rule applies if you decide to build a home, although then you are given an eighteen-month grace period after the sale within which to start living in it. Any capital expenditure on the building during the year before and the eighteen-month grace period is taken into account in assessing the cost of the house.

Remember that, whether buying or building, you have only postponed your liability. If you later decide to sell the new house, you will be confronted with a tax demand based on the original price of the old one.

There is one big exception to all this, but it will only apply to you if you decide to postpone selling your home until you are sixty-five. Anyone aged sixty-five or over is allowed $20,000 of the money from the sale, free of capital gain tax, so long as the seller has lived in the house for five years during the eight-year period before the sale.

Q: My wife and I are both thirty-six years old, and have five children. Three children will be in college at the same time, and we are trying to plan for their educations. We have $4,000 in savings; a $5,000 mortgage on our $50,000 home; and two pieces of rental property valued at $90,000. I carry $125,000 of life insurance and my annual income is $19,000. My plan is to refinance our home and use the equity as a down payment on another rental property, giving us additional income and a savings. Do you agree?

Mr. D. E. (Cincinnati, Ohio)

A: I do—but not just because you are overinvested in your home relative to your circumstances. One good reason for the practicality of your plan is that you will be doing more in the real estate business in which you have learned to do well. No one in your income bracket with five children—three of them in college—and with your standards and sense of responsibility—evidenced by the life insurance you carry—can hope to manage without developing a second source of income and working at it, as you are, by building up your rental property sideline. I hope your wife is learning how to work at it.

Q: I am sixty-two and my husband is fifty-nine. He is a veteran with a 60 percent disability, for which he receives $151 a month. He earns $8,000 a year. I receive Social Security of $87 a month, and we also have $2,000 in savings. Last year, we put almost $6,000 in a growth fund and also bought a four-unit apartment building with a 6 percent, twenty-five-year mortgage. We live in one unit and rent the other three, but the rents do not quite cover the cost of mortgage payments and upkeep. We wonder if our investments were wise.

Mrs. W. O. R. (Cincinnati, Ohio)

A: Don't blame your building if the rent from three-quarters of it doesn't quite cover its carrying costs. Calculate on the basis of whether it would show a profit if the fourth unit you occupy were a rent producer, too. By this test, your building investment looks pretty good.

I wish I could say the same about your growth fund. Your primary need is income, and a growth fund is a luxury you can't afford. You'll probably do better to keep the building, sell the fund, and settle for the going rate on savings. You are just kidding yourselves if you don't allocate the cost of rent for your own living quarters. How much would your rent cost you if you had to pay cash for it?

Q: On the principle that you stated in your syndicated newspaper column—that market values capitalize income —do you agree that the emergency freeze on rents suspends the case for property investment as a hedge against inflation?

Mr. I. C. (Hempstead, Long Island)

A: I would if I regarded the original freeze on rents as more than a public relations exercise which, in fact, it has not been. The loophole exemption leaving local governments free to continue hiking property taxes guaranteed the thawing which has developed for the rent freeze. Rent control formulae are being scrapped faster than they are being publicized. New York City's self-defeating experience with rent controls stranded it with the country's highest level of rents, as well as of abandonments. Continuation of the rent freeze would force higher abandonments and, consequently, higher rents and property values. The biggest long-term beneficiary of the immediate situation is likely to be land values on nonincome property.

Q: My mother is eighty years of age, does not own any property, and is interested in increasing her income. Her portfolio is substantial, and she has $9,000 in a savings ac-

count drawing 4½ percent interest. Any suggestions you can make will be appreciated.

Mrs. D. C. (Dearborn, Michigan)

A: The simple and safe way for your mother to increase her income is to take advantage of today's high yields on bonds by switching her stocks to bonds. Also, she has more money than time and can safely begin to live on her capital as fast as her convenience and health require, but as slowly as her peace of mind about security dictates.

Q: You often recommend real estate as an investment. But I wonder if you should not make it clear to your readers that real estate is not always the right place for investors, and never the right place for traders. In particular, I have in mind that the words "short term" applied to land investment commonly mean five to ten years, while it is something else again in the securities field. "Long term" to me means land bought with the intention of giving it to my grandchildren.

Mr. D. K. (Glenview, Illinois)

A: All your points are well taken. The prudence of any investment decision depends on the particular circumstances and aims of the investor; and it is likely to be as prudent as the investor is well advised.

If anything, your five- to ten-year time span is conservative as a short-term guideline for land investment. Your description of it as a "grandchildren's investment" is realistic. All property is inherently less marketable and less liquid than securities; and, therefore, calculations on the time span of property investment want to be very much longer than for securities investment. Also, the calculation on long-term gain wants to compensate for the sacrifice of income on the capital tied up waiting for the land to come into its own.

Q: In a recent column you mentioned property requiring no labor cost to maintain it as a defense against devaluation. What kind of property falls in this category?

Mrs. J. A. M. (Chicago, Illinois)

A: Land.

Q: I am seventy-nine, with no dependents or extraordinary living expenses. Due to an arthritic hip, I retired at sixty-six. My monthly income from Social Security and pension amounts to $251. My investments include $10,000 in bonds; 5,100 shares of stock; 412 shares in utilities; a $5,000 savings certificate; and $1,500 income from family property.

My concern is my late father's 127-acre farm in South Carolina. Land is good security, but I am physically unable to maintain it. I have been offered $750 an acre and have been advised to sell. What do you suggest?

Miss F. P. (St. Petersburg, Florida)

A: I'm not very optimistic about prospects for appreciation in working farm land. More money will be made by farm owners selling out to city developers than by working the land. In your circumstances, the money is worth more to you now than the land may be worth for non-farm use. I think the advice to sell is good.

Q: It seems that the worst is yet to come. During the depression, many farmers lost their farms. Our farm is 320 acres of good dairy land, worth $300 an acre. We owe $27,000 on a mortgage and $10,000 on cattle and machinery. We own two rental houses worth $14,000. Our taxes, mortgage payments, and loans are all going up. I am forty-six, with two teen-agers. If more bad times are ahead, would selling the farm and seeking city employment be wise?

Mr. R. Y. (Lebo, Kansas)

A: Worried though I have been, I do not believe that the foreclosure history of the last depression is about to repeat itself. Selling your farm and looking for a city job might not be your only alternative. For instance, the drop in farm prices is improving the demand for farm machinery. Have you given thought to trying to get a little cash by selling some machinery? I sometimes wonder whether we didn't buy more than we needed when times were good.

Even though you are making a go of your operation, another alternative might be for you to go to your local bank with the suggestion that it find you a buyer on condition that it also find you a deal managing a larger operation. In the world we live in today, management is commanding an ever higher marketplace premium; while owning property for the sake of owning property is no longer a paying proposition. Why not tell the banks in your area that you are available? Selling your farm or even leasing it to a tenant and going to work as a farm manager might be your answer.

Q: Land in our area is an attractive investment, but it doesn't have the liquidity of stocks. How would you suggest we balance our assets?

Mr. C. R. W. (Coeur d'Alene, Idaho)

A: Land is less liquid than stocks, but it offers a long-term gain potential that stocks, for the moment, no longer do. After all, the government cannot print land, but the peak of this bull market is going to see a great deal more printing of new stock certificates—all of them for sale.

Q: I have an opportunity to invest $10,000 in some good land in Alaska. There is a good chance of oil being on it, as some very successful drilling already is being done nearby. I have $5,000 in a Savings and Loan association at 5¼ percent. Should I use this amount and borrow the other $5,000 at 6½ percent? Or should I keep my $5,000 in reserve and borrow the whole $10,000?

Mr. F. E. N. (Aurora, Illinois)

A: The kind of speculation you describe is no proper use for borrowed money.

Q: My wife and I are in our mid-forties and are investing for retirement. My wife is employed, and I have substantial life insurance. Our reserve cash is close to the recommendations outlined in your book What Shall I Do With My Money? *Our $10,000 stocks are limited to a* *mortgage investment company, stock options from my employer, and a no-load growth mutual fund. We have invested in two orange groves in Florida. Potential income from the land might be around $4,000 a year. We are considering a third grove and will continue to add $1,000 annually to the fund. What do you think of the orange grove investment for long-term appreciation and income potential?*

Mr. E. W. (Naperville, Illinois)

A: Orange groves represent one form of betting on the weather, and this is speculative. While speculation has its place, as a use for mad money, and while orange groves can suit this purpose, I don't regard them as suitable for investment to build a retirement fund. Nevertheless, I could not be more optimistic about land values in Florida.

Q: Are real estate partnerships a good investment vehicle? I've been looking at a company which sells partnership units for $15,000 per unit in large apartment buildings. It's supposed to be a good deal.

My wife and I are both working. Would it be better for us to buy a house in a resort area? We could use it for vacations now and move there on retirement. Our present home is paid for.

Mr. J. O. (Hamilton, Ohio)

A: Caveat emptor is Latin for "buyer beware." Real estate that is merchandised in $15,000 units calls for this rule to be invoked. You and your wife would do better to think of any resort home you buy as strictly for use—provided you can afford it—not as an investment.

Q: The case you make for property investment sounds great—almost too good to be true. Can anything go wrong?

Miss S. H. (Mineola, Long Island)

A: You are right to ask. If Washington continues to fan inflation, the mid-1970s will bring on the danger of a serious collision in the mortgage market. Hundreds of millions of dollars of low-cost, "slow-pay" mortgages were written early in the postwar boom—mostly with payment schedules calling for big "balloon" payments (greater than the actual rate of pay-down) at maturity.

These maturities will fall due mainly on entrepreneur-owned apartment house developments—and, hence, will involve much larger sums than single-family homes. Thanks to the inflation in building and labor costs and property values, the mid-1970s will generate a "once-in-a-generation" jump of spectacular proportions in the country's need for new mortgage money. This means that the property market could be left vulnerable to a payments crisis if present policies and conditions persist.

The practical way to avoid being caught in any such mortgage refinancing crisis is to make sure that any property investment buys mortgage protection at least ten years ahead. This is still not hard to find.

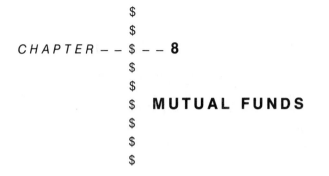

$
$
$
$
$ **MUTUAL FUNDS**
$
$
$

"**W**hat about mutual funds?" is a famous first question whenever the investment dollar comes up. The best answer recalls the old saying that you can't get anything out of a hat that you don't put into it. No mutual fund can do any better for you than the investments it makes do for itself.

In this era of inflation, the concept of investment performance has been inflated by the aggressive merchandising of certain johnny-come-lately mutual funds. The most relevant fact to bear in mind is that the mutual funds with the best and most consistent performance records were created before and during the depression, and have enjoyed a consistent rise since. A companion fact to bear in mind about the mutual funds which have worn best is that few of them have ever performed best in any given year. The contrast also points a sobering moral: few mutual funds which have outperformed the pack in any given year have ever managed to put anything like three outstanding years back to back. The rule for mutual funds is that consistency of good performance is bought at the price of spectacular but erratic performance. The prudent mutual fund investor is well advised to pay a price in performance sought by settling for consistency demonstrated.

The impressive growth of the mutual fund industry has brought with it a tendency to exaggerate its importance. It is important, but it is by no means the dominant force that it is sometimes said to be in institutional investment. The trust companies are very much larger.

Whereas today's mutual fund industry is only $50 billion big, the country's trust companies account for no less than $790 billion. Their management of pension funds guarantees to make them grow very much faster. They also enjoy the managerial advantage—it may work out as a performance disadvantage!—of not being required by federal regulation to operate in a goldfish bowl. Trust fund operations are not reportable as a matter of public information.

A certain amount of speculation has been invited by the evidence that the mutual fund business has been losing its growth characteristics. Some stock market speculators have taken to playing the market in anticipation of new placements of mutual fund shares with the amateur public—or, alternatively, redemptions by it. But the stock market has as little trouble in foiling such speculative game plans as it does in outsmarting the shorts. The fact that some mutual funds happen to be fully invested does not mean that all are. Nor does it mean that some better managed funds are not in comfortable cash positions and ready and able to take advantage of investment opportunities. Some of the better managed funds have built record backlogs of cash when their industry as a whole was reporting itself effectively out of cash. This is a reminder of how misleading statistics can be—especially overall statistics.

The key question is: which mutual fund is doing what, in pursuit of which policy, and in continuation of what performance? Perhaps the most troublesome and riskiest question raised for the investor in mutual funds has been occasioned by regulatory moves made in the name of protecting the mutual fund shareholder. As a practical matter, the combination of recent regulatory innovations and court rulings have taken the play out of the mutual fund business. Only anyone looking for a sinecure is now likely to enter the field or to be well-advised in trying. The new rules of the road, which have prompted shrewd investment advisers (known as brokers) to wonder if they are engaged in yesterday's business, are also squeezing the incentive out of the mutual fund business.

The new emphasis on protection for shareholders may end by hurting them more than it helps them. Prospective customers of mutual funds have more reason than ever to ask, "What's in it for management?" Unless mutual fund managers are likely to make more profit out of the fund than the shareholders do, the shareholders cannot be very sure of doing well. For if free advice is worth every cent of what it costs, the price of profitable advice is necessarily a rich profit to the adviser.

The mutual fund industry is a highly diversified one, with a wide choice of investment vehicles. Funds can be classified by objective, such as "growth" or "income." They can be classified by investment media, such as "specialty" funds, which concentrate on chosen industries (like chemicals, or aircraft, or energy, or insurance); or "balanced" funds, which invest in bonds as well as stocks. A new type of fund is directed at the advantages to be gained from investing in real estate. There are "closed-end" funds, the shares of which are limited: to buy them you must make a bid for shares from a present owner. "Open-end" funds issue new shares on demand at a price set by the value of the assets owned by the fund. There is also a distinction between "load" and "no-load" funds: the former take the sales charge when the shares are bought; the latter have no sales charge.

The switch in investor emphasis from stock-chasing to income-mindedness has given birth to still another type of fund: the bond fund. Some bond funds are closed-end vehicles and some are open end. In either case, the bond fund gives the investor in a diversified portfolio of bonds the opportunity to be a stockholder while enjoying the protection of owning bonds and getting income from them. The strategy of the bond fund is well hedged. When interest rates rise (and bond prices fall), they pay higher yields to the income-minded investor. When interest rates fall (and bond prices rise), they make trading profits and pay extra dividends on them.

When the next big switch from the present era of high interest rates starts, bonds bought at today's yields will be salable at very profitable premiums. At that time, bond funds will offer the income-minded investor—who is the prototype of the capital-conserving and profit-making investor—still a third hedge: playing convertible debentures. When the happy day for that big switch dawns, convertible debentures will offer the best of both worlds.

There are as many different kinds of mutual funds as there are alternative investment uses for your money. The law governing their regulation, policed by the Securities Exchange Commission, requires any mutual fund salesman to offer you your choice of three to insure that you pick one that fits your investment circumstances. Investing in mutual funds can only work as well as your thinking about them does.

The only sound approach to investing in mutual funds is for the long pull. Different kinds of funds are appropriate for investors with different requirements. No matter what the type of fund chosen, playing it for short-run speculative gain is the way to earn frustration and disappointment. For investors with a long view, mutual funds offer a prudent and proved means of transforming the surplus left from current income into a meaningful stock of capital.

Q: Each of our two children has just inherited $3,000. My husband wants to invest half of these sums in a mutual fund. I feel it would be safer to put the money into two-year savings certificates and accumulate the interest. This money is for our children's education and I am afraid of stocks.

Mrs. T. F. (Minneapolis, Minnesota)

A: I could tell you more if you could tell me if you and your husband have set aside either 10 percent of your annual income, or six months' living costs, in a savings reserve. If you have, you can feel free to invest all—not just half—of your children's inheritance in a mutual fund. Mutual funds are for long-term investment with money free from emergency pressures. They are ideal to finance the future education of youngsters. The safest and most profitable way to invest in them is to continue buying more when their market value is down. Bad markets enable investors to buy more shares for the same amount of cash —provided you limit your commitments to quality mutual funds with a proven record of performance. I think that you will buy a bigger headstart on the high cost of education—which now has a headstart over everyone—in mutual funds than in savings, provided that your children's money can be regarded as free to play the waiting game.

Q: I am thirty-seven, and my thirty-eight-year-old husband is in the 50 percent tax bracket. Our home is worth $75,000; we have $80,000 invested in educational bonds; and $40,000 in savings certificates. Early this year, I made a $9,000 profit in the market, and I am thinking of selling some of my bonds to offset the profit. I feel that our money would be safer in a conservative mutual fund, in view of our age, as a hedge against inflation. Do you agree?

Mrs. M. M. (Detroit, Michigan)

A: Yes. Funds are ideal for couples of your age who are able and willing to commit themselves for the long term. Make sure that the fund of your choice has a consistent, continuous record of performance. Also, that it did not enjoy a big bulge of new shareholders during the short-lived stock market surges of recent years.

The funds which did are subject to redemption pressures during market sinking spells. These redemption pressures have been forcing vulnerable "performance" funds to dump stocks in market storms which the conservative funds are able to weather.

Q: From reading your column, I get the impression that you are strongly against mutual funds. Why?

Mrs. J. W. (St. Cloud, Florida)

A: Stuff and nonsense. For years, I have caught brick-bats for "pushing" mutual funds. I still do, so long as the funds are proper investment funds, conservatively managed with an eye to the long pull, and not gambles on beating the market. I am against so-called performance funds. I am for bona fide investment funds.

Q: My son is a serviceman serving in the Philippines. He has been sending his money home, and I have invested $1,000 in what seemed a sound mutual fund. He is single, out of school and saving for the future. Should he continue investing in this fund even though it has not been doing well?

Mr. C. P. (Lawrenceville, Illinois)

A: In principle, yes. In practice, the problem plaguing all young people starting up in his position today is that $1,000 is no longer the meaningful sum it was in the early days of mutual fund investment. If he can continue to pool $1,000 a year, he will come out ahead eventually if he continues to use it to buy as many shares of this fund as $1,000 will buy, no matter how much lower the quotation may fall for a year or two. The term for this is dollar averaging.

Q: Will you please explain what the Keogh plan is?

Mr. J. C. (Palatine, Illinois)

A: Sponsored by former Congressman Eugene Keogh, it grants to professional people and the self-employed the right to set aside 10 percent of their income, or $2,500 a year—whichever is less—to go into a fund. The proceeds are tax-free until withdrawn at retirement. The funds can be set up through banks, insurance companies, or mutual funds.

Q: *My wife and I are both forty-six years old with a joint income of $16,000. Our assets include: $10,000 in Treasury notes; $5,000 in state bonds; $6,800 in a credit union; $4,000 in savings; and 10 shares of a mutual fund. Would you advise increasing our fund holdings and redistributing our other investments?*

Mr. R. B. (Williamsville, New York)

A: No. The way for a family in your circumstances and time of life to use mutual funds is by adopting a plan for regularly scheduled monthly investment, at a rate you can comfortably budget, over and above your cash reserve position. The alternative you suggest would deprive you of the benefit of your savings as a reserve. Keeping it intact will free you to start budgeting for investment.

Q: *I have $41,000 in mutual funds. This amount has been built up primarily by reinvestment of cash dividends and capital gains over the last fifteen years. I expect to retire in another year and will need supplemental income. Instead of reinvesting the dividends, would you advise taking the cash dividends and capital gains in cash and setting up a monthly withdrawal plan, or cashing in to buy an annuity or AAA bonds?*

Mr. R. H. (Clio, Michigan)

A: During your working prime, you used your mutual fund vehicles in the wisest way they can be used—for the systematic and steady accumulation of capital. But now that you will need more income instead of being able to afford the same input, the time is at hand for you to rethink your position.

A monthly withdrawal plan would keep most of your capital working for a low return and would defer the switch you need to expedite for a higher return on your capital.

Taking the annuity alternative would bet on your life expectancy. Medical advice may be more useful to you in making this decision than investment advice. Annuities pay off for investors who live long enough to get their money back plus a life income from the insurance company.

Your question does not mention the tax liability you will accrue as you cash in your funds. Bonds are your best bet. Ask the sponsor of the fund you have whether you can switch into a bond fund; and if you can, whether the switch can be effected on a tax-free basis. A bond fund would increase your income. A tax-free switch into the shares of a bond fund would defer your tax liability. Limiting your bond investments to AAAs sacrifices income you need for an extra margin of protection you don't need.

Q: Two years ago, I invested $50,000 in a mutual fund and have been receiving a monthly $200 withdrawal check. I am a sixty-five-year-old widow, and I use this money to supplement my income. I am now growing concerned about mutual funds.

Mrs. M. C. (Orlando, Florida)

A: In your circumstances, you need as much income as you can get, consistent with safety for your savings. Mutual funds will not give you maximum current income. Their purpose is different from yours. You apparently believe that your $200 withdrawal check represents income. You had better find out how much of it is a payback of your own money and how little of it is income. Even if it were all income, it would still come to under 5 percent— less than you could have been earning from a savings account without taking any risk.

But the unsuitability of your present holdings for your present needs does not justify your concern about mutual funds. The better-run mutual funds have earned investor confidence in their ability to weather periods of stress such as the present one.

Q: I own 812 shares of a conservative mutual fund worth around $11,000. I will retire in eight years. I am thinking of selling these shares. However, I am in the 50 percent tax bracket. The tax on my profit would be about $500. Would you advise selling?

Mrs. L. E. (Chicago, Illinois)

A: Think of the investment merits first, and the tax consequences second. As a practical matter, I have no doubt that conservative mutual fund portfolios will be worth considerably more when you reach retirement in 1979. You will do better to think less about selling and more about taking advantage of any market drop to buy more during your high-earning years.

Q: Over and above all the regulations we read about, how can the average, mature small-town investor, who has heard so many lurid stories about security sales mal-practices, be on guard against being taken by greedy mutual fund salesmen?

Mrs. M. J. (Redhook, Iowa)

A: The worst single security sales abuse, which no regulation can reach, is the practice called "churning." This describes what salesmen do to chalk up commissions at the expense of their customers' capital.

Once fund buyers have paid the "load" charge, the very worst thing that can happen to them is to be fast-talked into liquidating the holding and being switched into another load fund, absorbing another sales load charge. Unscrupulous salesmen have been known to clip customers in this way more than twice in one year.

The SEC has been able to reach and to regulate the companion practice of churning portfolios at the management level as a safeguard to fundholders against netting inordinate brokerage fees.

Q: Have I missed your opinion of closed-end funds? They appear to me to be a bargain when bought at minus 10, or more, and held for the long term.

Mr. H. S. (Gary, Indiana)

A: They are when bought on this basis. The question is whether they can ever be sold on any other kind of basis. Be wary of putting yourself in the position of the fellow who thought he had discovered the wheel centuries after everyone had been using it. The word about the discount on closed-end funds has been old hat for decades. No one is about to make a quick buck turning them over on sales at premiums to suckers.

The new breed of closed-end bond funds are not quoted at discounts under their breakup value. Nevertheless, they offer a better deal to stock buyers interested in income and willing to hold them for income.

Q: I am just now fifty-eight years old and my children are married. My wife and I are wondering about the best type of investment for the future. I expect to work at least ten to fifteen years more, which is altogether possible in my profession.

I understand there are certain mutual funds that do not charge a percentage for their services. Would you recommend this type of investment? We are interested in growth.

Rev. P. V. (Cincinnati, Ohio)

A: You are referring to "no-load" funds. Their sponsors impose no sales charge. They do pay management fees themselves, but do not pass the cost directly on to the customer. Instead, a cash charge is made on the assets of the fund.

But it's the past record of a fund you should look at when considering it as an investment. Whether it is a "load" or a "no-load" fund, it is performance that matters. A "no-load" fund that loses half your capital is more expensive than a "load" fund that charges you up to 8 percent on the way in, makes it back for you in a reasonable period of time—measured in years, not weeks—and conserves your capital instead of dissipating it.

Don't generalize about either "load" or "no-load" funds. As Al Smith used to say, "Look at the record." One way of assessing the performance of the best load funds is to discount the loss of the first year's income as well worth a trade-off for substantial capital appreciation over the long-term period for which the investment is to be held.

One charge you should watch out for, however, is a performance fee which some funds take out as an incentive for their managers. Private advisers try to play this game, too, but don't you get involved in it. Such incentives led in 1967–68 to serious abuses of sound investment practice in pursuit of day-to-day performance.

Q: I am a fifteen-year-old boy. I deliver the Detroit Free Press *and earn about $8 a week. I would like to invest my earnings, but don't know where.*

Won't you please tell me what to do? I want to get into a planned program that will take me through the next twenty years, starting now.

Mr. M. R. B. (Mount Clemens, Michigan)

A: More power to you. Hope I'm around twenty years from now to ask your advice.

Tell one of the local investment dealers to pick out a conservative closed-end bond fund for you. Put a fixed amount into it every three months. Your monthly dividend will yield you over 7 percent. I expect that it will yield you more after a while. When you get it, put it in the bank until enough builds up to buy more shares. Meanwhile, get an extra benefit out of your high school math course by familiarizing yourself with a compound interest table. It will be working for you as steadily as you are working for yourself.

Q: I disagree with your recent advice to invest $10,000 from the sale of a home in a mutual fund instead of in 5 *percent savings certificates. The $10,000 will purchase only $9,200 in market value of securities.*

Income might net $460 a year after deducting management fees, and tax obligations would accrue on dividends and capital gains. But $10,000 invested in 5 percent savings certificates would return $500 a year without cost of any kind, and not subject to market depreciation.

Mr. A. H. F. (Fort Lauderdale, Florida)

A: Dissent and debate are the tools of decision-making. I appreciate your helpful counterarguments. Herewith rebuttals.

Your complaint seems to be directed against the purchase of high-load funds, at any time. But the "load" paid in sales charges buys professional management. If the return which professional management earns for the amateur investor *over a period of time* doesn't more than pay for the sales charges, the answer is to buy better management. The boom-and-slump market of recent years has provided investors with the opportunity of judging competitive track records in good times and bad.

By the way, you'll do well to remember that the interest earned on savings certificates does bear a cost, too—the cost of tax payments at ordinary income rates. Year in and year out, any professional management worth its keep can accrue a higher net return on capital in the form of appreciation than the after-tax return on savings certificates—that's the difference between savings and investment, about which you are confused.

I have never advocated mutual fund investment as a way of beating the market on fast turns, or for people who don't have time and patience for the long pull. The younger and more amateurish the investor, the better suited funds are for keeping what's in the basket protected while getting it carried. Investors who have stayed with the best mutual funds over a period of years are now receiving annual cash yields on their original investments substantially in excess of the 5 percent now tempting you.

Q: My wife and I are both retired and want to invest $10,000 of our savings. We have often seen you recommend mutual funds in your syndicated column, but I don't think you have ever commented specifically on ones dealing exclusively in government securities. We would like to benefit from the higher returns on short-term government securities and are thinking of investing our money in this type of fund. What is your opinion?

Mr. N. P. H. (Riverside, Illinois)

A: Since you are both retired, prudence dictates that you limit your risk. I think the fund choice you are minded to make is a good one. The yield based on last year's dividend was about 6.8 percent on the current market price, and I would think the safety of your investment is assured. But bond funds not limited to owning governments are returning higher yields. In my opinion, they are subject to less risk of capital depreciation than funds limited to governments.

Q: I was approached about a program which featured mutual funds packaged with life insurance. The life insurance premiums would be paid by a loan secured with the fund shares as collateral, with no repayment of principal or interest on the loan for ten years, at which time the note is due in full and is paid by liquidating some of the mutual fund shares.

Would you please comment on this concept, because it sounds almost too good.

Mr. J. A. (Winnetka, Illinois)

A: Your question is an accurate summary of a concept which has been institutionalized and merchandised for some time. The gamble is on how well the mutual fund may do during the ten-year period. You could be stuck with the difference between the value of the fund shares and what you owe the bank at the end of the period.

Q: I am retired. It is my desire to invest $10,000 in bonds which will give me at least 7 percent interest with maximum security. My thought was to purchase an AAA-rated utility bond, such as AT&T.

The broker I have consulted recommends that I invest in his "bond mutual fund" which will permit him to take a commission of 8½ percent, or $850, from my $10,000. His reasoning, which I do not entirely understand, is that this will give me diversification and professional management.

How do you see these two procedures? I lean to the single AAA-rated corporate bond with the much smaller commission. Could this entail greater risk?

Mrs. R. B. S. (St. Petersburg, Florida)

A: You are right to resist your broker. Top-rated bond funds are available as closed-end mutual funds, salable without delay for computation or redemption and at regular commission—like any other stock exchange security. You can ask him to buy you a closed-end bond fund, yielding over 7 percent, with the dividend payable monthly. Or you can buy an AA-rated or even A-rated bond: you would neither pay a premium for safety you don't need nor risk a default on interest, and could get a return of better than 7 percent.

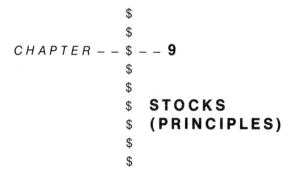

CHAPTER – – $ – – 9

$ STOCKS
$ (PRINCIPLES)

By far the most important influence inside the stock market relates to its dependence on the vital axis that connects Washington and Wall Street. In its new-era role as the carrier of government pressures and policies, the stock market is the sector of the economy most sensitive to changes of emphasis in governmental operations.

In *What Shall I Do With My Money?*, I urged acceptance of this still unfamiliar premise that the primary influence on the stock market is not economic but financial and political. The increasingly sharp swings of the market since then—responsive, in every case, to political stimulus—have confirmed this judgment.

Nevertheless, no single, simplistic formula ever fits as an explanation of stock market action. Market moves result from the continuing interplay of at least three interacting factors. Actual changes in money conditions are the first. Expected changes in business conditions are the second. Changes in political bets are the third.

The stock market can and will strengthen during the worst of recessions—provided only that government is seen coming to the rescue and, just as important, trusted to be effective in its remedial efforts. Contrariwise, when both the economy and the stock market are strong, they can become vulnerable to government incantations and crackdowns aimed at potential excesses—especially when, at critical turning points from confidence in boom to fear of bust, government's efforts hit the target of overkill.

But the record of the market itself demonstrates that the great swings of stock market confidence—defying current drops and surges in earnings—reflect changes in political and financial conditions. The most influential of these is the pressure exerted by government on financial conditions, measured by the alternate easing or tightening of money conditions.

Everyone knows about the constitutional system of checks and balances responsible for the dual sovereignty over money in which Congress participates as an equal partner with the President and his appointees. Its success depends upon the President's ability to deal with Congress. But the financial consequences of this system vary with the relative solvency or bankruptcy of the executive establishment centered in the White House.

The birth of the great bull market of the postwar era was delayed but not aborted when President Harry S. Truman took up the cudgels against Senator Robert A. Taft and "the do-nothing, good-for-nothing 80th Congress" of 1946–48. As that memorable chapter of political history proved, no President can lose a war of words with Congress while the government over which he presides is solvent, and while the taxpayers over whom he governs are comfortable and confident. During that era of affluence, money was a giveaway. The government had plenty of it and, even more important, its customers—the taxpayers—had more cash and access to more credit than they knew what to do with.

The death of the postwar bull market saw repeated but unsuccessful efforts to resurrect it—but with a difference. First President Johnson and, then, President Nixon learned that no President can hope to win a war of words with Congress while presiding over a crisis of government finance in Washington, and despite a failure of nerve among the taxpayers. A Presidential try at it is as futile as the town deadbeat railing at the sheriff. A President on bad terms with Congress can hope to manage only if he can borrow less, rather than more; and only if he needs to raise less in taxes rather than more.

The post-depression generation of boom in American history has long since reversed the cynical and truculent "know-nothingism" expressed by President Roosevelt's man Friday, Harry Hopkins, who boasted that the New Deal would "spend and spend, tax and tax, and elect and elect." Nowadays, freedom from fear on the part of the political "ins" that they will not get re-elected swings with their freedom from the need to borrow more and to tax more in order to cover their overspending. More than politics is involved in the test of political confidence as the first principle of stock market strength. The rate of interest measures it.

Back when President Truman was waging his "sure-thing" war of words against Senator Taft, the rate of interest was fluctuating between negative and nominal. Labor was already asserting its right to regard negotiation as a catch-up dividend on its having gone along with wage controls during the war years. But payment for the use of money, represented by the rate of interest, was still worth next to nothing and still not getting more expensive. As I recall joking at the time, robbing banks had suddenly become uneconomic: accommodating them by signing notes for the loans they were anxious to make at giveaway interest rates was easier work and less risky. Dividend yields, by contrast, were generous but not appreciated.

The yield spread is the first test of stock market strength. It represents the money measure of political confidence in the President's chances of winning or losing any war of words with the money power represented by Congress. It measures not merely the rate of inflation, but the influence of inflation in at once bidding investment money out of stocks and deflating investor confidence. When the dividends paid on stocks yield more than the interest paid on bonds, the dividend interest spread is said to be positive. So long as this remains true, stocks will go up despite any lack of confidence investors may have.

The other side of the coin from a positive yield spread (underwriting political confidence as the motive power of investor confidence) is a negative yield spread. Any time the yield spread is negative, interest rates on bonds yield more than dividend payouts on stocks because big government has needed more money than it has had. The negative yield spread is the reliable measure of the President's resultant loss of influence with Congress.

During such spells of negative yield spreads, high levels of business borrowings threaten to precipitate competitive scrambles for money between business and government. Although inflation control is the government's professed aim during such money squeezes, its real intent is to get rid of private sector competition, able (as it is not) to cut its net interest rate in half as a tax deduction. Pragmatically, intervals of government crackdown against accelerations in business borrowing bring new lows for investor confidence, and for political confidence as well. For the message they carry is at one and the same time an effective threat to business commitments. The willingness of business to commit capital, and of Congress to cooperate with the Executive, stem from the same roots. Investor confidence is the other side of the coin from political confidence.

The professionals who make a business of daily stock market dealings are really no different from anyone else in business. They need customers. The customers who make the difference between a strong and weak stock market are the members of the amateur money-using public, who save their money when they are scared to invest it, and who invest it only when they are not scared to save it.

A constant running test of market strength or weakness is provided by evidence of the accumulation of blocks or, alternatively, distribution. Accumulation guarantees market strength. By the same token, distribution brings on market weakness. The workings of the oldest law of economics—none other than the age-old law of supply and demand—explains it. The process of accumulation squeezes the supply of good stocks, sending their prices up. The accumulators invariably concentrate on the good stocks as their targets for accumulation.

Contrariwise, the process of distribution overloads the market's absorptive capacities. Ironically, the process of accumulation invariably strengthens the market most when the participation of the public in it is greatest. Perversely, the process of distribution weakens it most when the mass departure of the public is hurting it the most. More than coincidence is involved. The accumulators of blocks have the confidence, and the buying power, to bid small holdings out of the hands of small holders who are swarming into the market. They worry about their exposure to forced liquidation when small holders are swarming out of the market, narrowing its base.

The stock market is strong when it is big, and weak when it is small. The key to the seeming enigma of Wall Street in 1972 was in the daily figures on volume of the shares traded. I suggested that, for the market to be strong, it would have to trade upward of 15 million shares a day, and to do so recurrently. Alternatively, I warned that a daily trading pattern of less than 15 million shares a day would result in a weak market.

By contrast, new highs in daily trading peaks of 25 million shares a day, without leading the market to new price highs, signaled the freezing of the market's strategic liquidity rather than its utilization as a propellant. The amateur money-using public held the balance of market power. Only its decision to flock back en masse from savings accounts and bonds could make the market big enough again to regain its strength.

"Intra-day" is a parallel performance test for professional stock market students training to judge the daily ebb and flow of trading strengths and weaknesses. The average stock market follower is content to keep track of what the market does each day or each week simply by noting whether it finishes up or down. The professionals pay more than normal attention to how it fares between each day's start and finish.

The intra-day test is particularly useful when the apparently decisive trend of the market is suspect. It was during the climactic phase of the great 1972 rally. And it will continue to be a measure of the likely strength of buying pressures needed to keep a rally moving. As fast as "up" days invite sellers to offer blocks each morning, buyers demand and get concessions for accommodating them. So long as the market is able to regain its momentum after and as blocks have been distributed, the most suspect of rallies will be on. But the moment the intra-day test begins again to register midday levels higher instead of lower than the daily closing, a rally is ready to be broken up.

The intra-day test works just as reliably in reverse as an early warning signal that market breaks are running their course and headed for recovery. The intra-day test turns positive when morning downticks are turned into closing upticks even though each day's closing may be lower than the last.

In the short run, the most influential test of the dominant professional attitude toward the prevailing trend of the market is the breadth index. The breadth index is just as simple as the intra-day test, but more fundamental. All it does is tell whether more stocks are going up each day, and vice versa. The point at which the breadth index turns negative, and where the intra-day test reveals unsustained highs for each trading day, marks the spot where a rally falters and fails.

A word may be in order on 1971's so-called Janeway Break of November 1—the talk was prompted by an interview published that day in *The New York Times* suggesting 500 as a likely 1972 test level for the Dow Industrial Average. I would like to think that the next time

I cite 2,000 as a likely target—and I was the first to cite it before the market reached it—the response will be as sensitive.

Meanwhile, notwithstanding my sense of alarm over the prospective fate of the market in its efforts to break out of its trading range and to stabilize itself on new high ground above its old high of 1,000, I have chided the unrealism of the bullish consensus for its willingness to settle for a mere restabilization of the market at that level. My New Year's greeting to 1972 was expressed in the Janeway Service of January 5—and again on CBS on January 8, and yet again to the Executives Club of Chicago—in the form of the assurance that, given a forward move to confidence-inspiring government policies, the market could and would offer better value to investors at its prospective new highs of 2,000 on the Dow Jones Average than back down where it was headed during the great 1972 rally.

Q: What do you think the eventual effect of wage and price controls is likely to be on the stock market?

Mr. F. K. (Villa Park, Illinois)

A: The need for controls generally hurts the stock market more than honeymoon hopes of their effectiveness can help it. The very fact that the need for Phase Two was admitted during month one of Phase One is proof that the emergency is continuing, and that the controls adopted have not yet come to grips with the problems of the emergency.

A still more specific reason why the new controls hurt the stock market is that the stock market has become increasingly volatile, representing a bet on political stunts as a substitute for the solution of economic problems. Meanwhile, the hard arithmetic to which President Nixon's New Economic Program has added up measures a sharpening squeeze on cost-dividend calculations to do with stocks. Phase Two has permitted the wage-cost push to resume, while retaining the prejudicial pressure against increases in dividends. But over any period of time, the prices of stocks capitalize the yields on the dividends they are free to pay. The sharpening cost squeeze would be closing off the hope that responsible corporations might earn and pay higher dividends, even if the controls set up were not prohibiting them from doing so.

1972's turn-of-the-year rally in the stock market reflected a Wall Street bet that the economy would restabilize itself in time to justify a pre-election proclamation by President Nixon of the emergency's end. Instead, the evidence is undeniable that the inflationary crisis is still with us, and that the controls system is here to stay until the authorities in Washington learn how to make it work. The longer controls stay in effect, the dimmer the prospect will be for stock prices. The only prospect that would be worse would be a premature decontrol move while the controls that had been adopted still need to be made to work.

Q: You have indicated in the past that inflation is the enemy of the stock market, and does not lead to higher prices. I agree with this idea over the short term. But I also believe that, over the long term, it is inflation that accounts for most of the price increases not only of the stocks of companies that have shown little real growth,

but of much of the price increases of growth companies.
Please comment.

Mr. P. J. (Chicago, Illinois)

A: Your question, as put, jumbles horses and apples. Inflation ends by eroding the growth rate of companies. But it begins by inflating the prices of stocks because buyers with money to back up their theories are willing to bid higher on optimistic expectations.

Higher prices paid for stocks earning less involve the buyers in a dilemma. If they are genuine investors for the long term, they are obliged to wait longer than expected for the earnings they anticipate to pay them going dividend returns.

Alternatively, if they are speculators, they are dependent on still more enthusiastic inflation buffs to bid stock prices still higher in order to give them a chance to cut and run at a profit.

The more the market bets on inflation, the more impatient the players become for quick profits. This means that, contrary to your presumption, inflationary psychology inflates stock prices in the short term, but exposes them to deflation in the long term.

Q: Would lower interest rates help the stock market?

Miss E. O. (Salt Lake City, Utah)

A: They always do—for so long as they are trusted to remain in force. Of course, inflation goes with higher interest rates, which is one of the reasons why it also brings lower stock prices.

Q: The dollar devaluation will not only hasten the market drop you have talked about but it will cause a more severe drop than anticipated. Also, inflation will worsen as a result of the devaluation. My position is to stay in cash or top-grade corporate bonds. I am thirty-nine, no debts and above average income. What do you think of my program?

Mr. C. K. (Milwaukee, Wisconsin)

A: You may be right about the stock market and your own investment program, but for the wrong reasons. A successful devaluation of the international dollar probably would have put the market up—this is how the last devaluation worked under Franklin Roosevelt.

Instead, devaluation expectations were first complicated and then frustrated. The failure of devaluation to pay off as expected suggests that 1971's post-Thanksgiving Day rally not only got way ahead of itself but made a turn in the wrong direction. Apart from this detail of our disagreement about the what and the why of what has been happening, I agree with your program.

Q: In November 1970, I wrote to you asking whether you agreed with stock brokers who were predicting 900 on the Dow. You told me then that the 1970 rally was the biggest bear rally since 1930, and not to follow the brokers' optimism. The country's economic problems do seem to support your view. Yet the market remains confident. Surely it can keep rising so long as investors support that confidence. The institutions are doing so, and I am thinking of following their example with $35,000 of

*my cash. Do you agree? Or do you still think I should
stay cool and leave the market alone?*

Mrs. F. M. (Chattanooga, Tennessee)

A: I certainly do not agree, and neither do the responsible fund managers in the investment business. The rate at which the market moved above 900 on the Dow saw its investment leadership downgraded and its speculative leadership brought to the fore. They have been hoping for a correction in time to cool off the speculation which is a sure-fire preliminary to a major break.

I question your confidence in the confidence of the market. It has seemed to me to be increasingly mistrustful of its own claims and projections. Not very much sophistication is needed to support the suspicion that a 1972 boom which admits the likelihood of a 1973 bust will begin to anticipate it. Most of the professionals who have been talking for publication about Dow Jones highs of 1,100 to 1,200 have been saying privately that they have no intention of waiting to unload until the market gets there. The riskiest market atmosphere of all is one in which the professionals are intent on outsmarting and out-trading each other while private investors remain on the sidelines unsatisfied by the yields stocks pay and promise to pay. By all means, keep your cool and your money.

*Q: For many years I have balanced my yield and
growth objectives by owning General Motors and du
Pont stock. Both companies have a well-established tradition of paying extra year-end dividends in addition to*

their regular quarterly dividends. Do you read the new freeze as banning regularized extra dividends?

Mr. F. P. (Richmond, Virginia)

A: I do not. Of course, the President has conceded that the government lacks the power to freeze dividends, and he was explicit in requesting voluntary compliance in the interest of avoiding any sense of unfair play. I cannot imagine that any major corporation will not be responsive to the President's request.

But I do not believe that the stockholders of GM and du Pont, and any other corporations and mutual funds with a normalized pattern of paying dividends on a dual basis, need worry about anything but the earning power behind their dividends.

All mutual funds are authorized by the Investment Company Act of 1940 to pay their dividends on a dual basis—regular on an income basis, plus interim on a gains basis.

Q: I retired a year ago, am sixty-eight, and my income is from Social Security, interest on investments, and interest from an S & L association. I am liquidating my municipal bonds as they mature, and I sold my stocks at a loss when they were higher than they are now, converting to corporate and utility bonds. I have $75,000 in savings, waiting for interest rates to rise. I have not bought a single stock since last year, waiting for the market to drop back below 800. Do I continue to wait for this drop or do I begin to buy now?

Mr. H. H. (Oshkosh, Wisconsin)

A: Your question is academic. It also recalls the experience of 1929's realists who got hurt going back into stocks too soon in 1931. I do not regard 800 as being close to bottom. Wait. You have shown good judgment not only to take your stock market losses when you did, but also to limit your buying of tax-exempt bonds to short-term maturities.

Q: You have stated that the market may go as low as 500 in 1972–73. Recently you advised a reader to wait until the market was lower than 800. I am getting nervous about when to jump back into the market. What will be the general trend of the market in the coming months?

Mr. R. K. (Tallahassee, Florida)

A: Bear market rallies tend to be sharper than bull market advances. Consequently, they generally seem more tempting—the closer to topping out and breaking up, the more tempting. Notwithstanding the optimism generated by 1971's year-end rally, which seemed literally topless at the time, hindsight saw the Dow Jones Average reach a significant resistance point. My expectation is that hindsight will show that the 1972 market ended in admittedly weaker shape than it started.

When 1971's year-end rally got started, it still had a great deal to look forward to—the success of the dollar devaluation; the continuation of low interest rates; the improvement in the economy; and, above all, the ability of the Nixon administration to underwrite a bull market strong enough in turn to underwrite his re-election. 1972's events successively turned each of these bets into an increasingly chancy speculation.

Q: For the first time in years, a number of my business and social acquaintances have told me of all the money they are making and expect to continue making on flyers in the stock market. Do you think I am an old stick-in-the-mud to be resisting the temptation to get with it and, instead, to be staying with my short-term tax-exempts and my cash reserve in the banks? I am not quite fifty years old.

Mr. S. T. (Gainesville, Georgia)

A: Absolutely not. While it is true that a return of amateur investor participation in the stock market is an indispensable precondition to its regaining its health, the talk you are hearing reflects amateur speculation. Genuine investment participation by the public is dividend-minded when it occurs, not speculative. A rise in amateur speculation is generally a telltale warning of a return to market trouble. The stock market almost never gets into trouble without such a speculative buildup. Trouble invariably follows when amateurs start chasing stocks they know nothing about and brag about catching them.

Q: I want to sell out my holdings in the stock market because I believe it is going to go down even more when the war is over and unemployment gets worse. Although I would have to take a loss if I sold out now, do you think it would still be a good idea?

Mr. M. P. (St. Petersburg, Florida)

A: I don't agree with your premise. If the war really were over, and the inflationary pressures it has unleashed were behind us, I have every confidence that unemployment could and would be soaked up.

Answering your question, however, I think that your instinct is sounder than your logic. After all, the stock market does not owe you your money back. Waiting until you are even can be as tricky as playing for the top dollar while you are ahead.

Q: In view of your forecast of a Dow drop to 500 in 1972–73, what is wrong with the investment strategy of gradual accumulation of Dow stocks before the averages drop to 500, in anticipation of the eventual rise to 1,500 or 2,000?

Mr. J. W. (Evanston, Illinois)

A: Nothing—this is, provided you have enough backup cash and sit-still fortitude to continue investing a budgeted monthly allotment of cash until the present decline hits bottom. You'll end up owning more shares of cheaper stocks and making more money than anyone trying to beat the market. I assume you plan to start slowly—by commiting only 5–10 percent of your kitty.

Just make sure that the Dow stocks you accumulate will survive in the Dow Index when the brewing storm is over. There already have been a number of casualties; and there will be more. One way to be sure is to extend your plan to include the Dow Jones utility stocks. I expect them to be the leaders of the next trustworthy upturn.

Q: I am seventy-five years old and have a small annuity plus Social Security, so am not wholly dependent on investment income. But I am afraid of the market going down and staying down for years. Do you think I should sell? If so, what should I do with the money?

Miss G. P. (*Chicago, Illinois*)

A: At your time of life, and in your circumstances, conservation of capital is your number one problem. Even if I were optimistic or, at worst, complacent about the stock market, I would recommend your clearing out altogether. You are unfair to yourself in committing your old age security to stocks at a time when even the market enthusiasts admit that a 10 percent rise in 1972 would be big; and when none of them deny that a much bigger drop is likely for 1973.

Q: I am a widow who is "running scared." I own a home worth about $41,000, have around 2,134 shares of utility and auto stocks, plus $10,000 in bonds, and $39,000 in savings accounts. Is there any safe way to get out of the stock market? The whole situation makes me a little dizzy.

Mrs. J. S. (*Lake Orion, Michigan*)

A: Just because it does, ask yourself if there's any safe way for anyone in your circumstances to stay in the stock market under present circumstances. Balancing your peace of mind against your hope of reward and your risk of gain argues for you to stop "running scared" in the market and to pull back to the security of the sidelines. As to your specific holdings, both the utility and the auto industries face more problems than opportunities. For the short term, at any rate, owning them is not for widows. Stocks never are when bonds yield more.

Q: I am fifty-seven, and run an engineering consulting business. My wife is a school teacher—thank goodness—and we have two children, one in her first year of college earning part of her way, and the other in high school, but already earning and saving for college. Our problem is that my wife and I are badly behind in our retirement programs and I want to conserve the other assets we have. These include $5,000 savings; $6,000 in stocks now only worth $5,000; $10,000 in Treasury bills and adequate insurance. We own our $15,000 home but are thinking of mortgaging it to pay our part of the college expenses. We've only held back because of the poor condition of my business and the talk of a depression.

Our stocks are only yielding 4 percent on their original cost—with the exception of a Japanese issue which has gained 40 percent in value since 1968. Would it be best to sell out the low-yielding stocks and hold on to this one successful investment? Or will that eventually be affected by world trade problems? I'm thinking of putting the money into high-yielding bonds.

Mr. G. V. (Palos Park, Illinois)

A: You have answered your own question. Taking a 40 percent profit in a Japanese stock is better than running the risk of waiting to take a 40 percent loss. In calculating the vulnerability of the stocks you own to the renewed rise in bond yields, you will do well to consider the yields their dividends pay—not at your cost, but at current market prices. You will also do well to try to ascertain how safe their present dividend payouts are. A return to 8 percent bond yields argues for investors to sell stocks they are not prepared to hold for a long pull.

Q: Recently you wrote about the relationship between the breadth index and the Dow Jones Averages, and how one influenced the other. Could you elaborate?

Mr. C. W. (Cincinnati, Ohio)

A: Think of a pyramid with the breadth index being its base and the Dow being its apex. A narrowing base is not likely to support a rising pyramid. Little wonder that the breadth index leads the Dow. It certainly did during the failure of 1971's summer rally. A falling breadth index and a rising Dow are standard features of the climactic breakup of a top-heavy market.

Q: I am writing to you to express my dismay at your continued, unbridled pessimism regarding the economy of this country. Do you not realize that this pessimism can do much to bring about the very depressed state of affairs you fear? Someone in your position has a definite influence over a wide segment of the investing public. Is it not more constructive to the future of our economy to stress what is right about it, thus helping to stabilize the atmosphere, than to be a prophet of gloom and doom?

After all, there are many thousands of investors, large and small, who stand to lose money every time one like yourself speaks of disaster. Your words contribute to a loss of confidence, which in turn causes the stock market to fall.

Mrs. N. P. (Detroit, Michigan)

A: Public relations are no substitute for the solution of economic and financial problems. I could not be more mindful of my responsibilities—the first of which is, as the youngsters remind us, to "tell it like it is"; and, as we oldsters of my generation have reason to recognize, to avoid opening plausibility gaps. I also have a vivid recollection of having been warned repeatedly not so long ago —when I was derided for my optimism as an "astronomic statistician"—that the encouragement I gave investors to make commitments with their savings exposed them to losses.

On the merits, the strongest affirmation of strength that a stock market can give results from its ability to take selling in stride. One of the most confidence-inspiring principles of market performance recognized in the marketplace is the so-called "contrarian" principle—that the pessimism of advisers builds a durable foundation of strength under the stock market. We can be thankful for this principle because it encourages the fundamental principle of free expression in what the late, great Mr. Justice Holmes spoke of as the "marketplace of ideas." Its vibrance is the indispensable precondition of confidence and strength for the entire economy and its markets.

No warnings of mine have in any way at any time expressed a lack of confidence in the unrivaled potential of the productivity of the American economy or of its leadership role. On the contrary, all of my warnings have been aimed at failures of policy on the part of the governmental managers. My specific warnings for the immediate future of the stock market have been even more specifically aimed at the bets being made in Wall Street that the government policies which have made problems for the economy would solve them. There's nothing wrong with the American economy that simple policies calculated to get it moving again would not quickly set right.

Q: Our life savings, $20,000, are in the bank and we own our home. In the next six years our two children will enter college. How can we help our kids through school and safely earn more than 4½ percent? We followed your advice and bought the 8 percent Treasury notes back when interest rates were still high. Should we get into the market?

Mrs. R. D. (Evanston, Illinois)

A: Good for you. You have had a profit all the way, together with your higher-than-market yield.

4½ percent is a low-yield target even though interest rates have been falling. Safe bonds are still yielding close to 7½ percent, which I regard as too low for long-term investment.

I do not regard a sky-rocketing stock market rally as a good time to invest—especially 1972's political rally. I would wait to see how high the dividend yields on well-covered utility stocks rise in the wake of bond yields responding to the inflationary revelation that the government's borrowing needs will stay up in the stratosphere. If the Dow utility stock average makes a new low in the spring, the time to start might be drawing close. Safe dividends bought right to yield high are the best bet for your family's educational purpose. Meanwhile, keeping your money in a savings account won't cost you any return.

Q: I agree with you that the stock market is too high for its own good and that it has been dangerously inflated by overspeculation in low-grade highflyers. I note that an increasing number of commentators agree that low-grade leadership is a danger signal.

Do you think this is the time to sell a few of these touted leaders short?

Mr. M. T. C. (New York, N. Y.)

A: Absolutely not. The only stocks it is ever relatively safe to "short" in anticipation of a big market top are big, stable ones, protected by a large, floating supply against the danger that the market makers will engineer a shortage. Tired markets are again and again refreshed when the professionals catch the amateurs in a short squeeze in "hot" little stocks.

Q: My husband is a doctor with a two-man medical corporation. He is setting up their corporation pension-profit sharing plan, involving some $30,000 this year. These are tax-deferred funds, and he would like to invest them wisely. I agree with you on getting out of the market, yet mutual funds are being pushed. What would be our best bet?

Mrs. F. G. (Rockford, Illinois)

A: Your questions about the market and mutual funds are too general to help your problem. The main advantage offered by private pension-profits plans is that of compounding income tax-free. Investment in safe, high yields—using stocks as well as bonds—is your best bet.

Q: I work for a manufacturer of an essential household item, whose president is a close relative. Although young, the firm is showing extraordinary growth and is considering going public. Do new issues usually go up or down at first? Or does this vary at the same rate as established stocks?

Mr. M. B. (Skokie, Illinois)

A: Market conditions determine the answer to both questions. When the market in unseasoned new issues is strongest, the market for established issues is generally closer to turning weak. An overebullient new issue market is a reliable, early warning that speculative capers are getting ahead of investment calculations.

Is "keeping up with the Joneses" the reason your relative is inclined to take his company public? If his company is doing so well, why would it make sense for him to share the wealth? Why doesn't he try first to raise money privately? In recent years, the road to distress for many flourishing family businesses has been paved with speculation on going public.

Q: I am an employee at a major auto plant earning $10,000, and I expect to retire in ten years. I am in the company stock plan which allows me to put in 10 percent of my gross income. Half of the money goes into govern-

ment bonds and the company equals the other half in stock. Considering the hard times we are in, I'm not sure whether this is the safest way to handle my money. What do you suggest?

Mr. H. H. (Detroit, Michigan)

A: Stay put. The right to participate in the type of plan you're in is one of the best reasons for working for a big company with an enlightened management. These plans are safe. You could not hope to do nearly as well for yourself as the plan is doing for you.

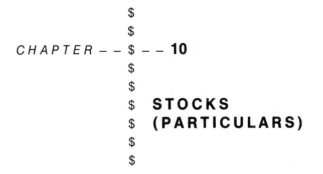

$
$
CHAPTER – – $ – – 10
$
$
$ **STOCKS**
$ **(PARTICULARS)**
$
$

Again and again, the first reaction of the securities markets to extreme surprise has been to go off in the direction exactly opposite to the one it will eventually take. The most conspicuous example—before August 15, 1971—was their misreading of the Russian achievement in launching Sputnik. Although this was the signal of a new era of expansion, the stock market broke. Not long after, however, it realized its fear was mistaken, and started up and away again.

Majority market opinion failed to anticipate the onset of the summer 1971 crisis. Then its first reaction was to reach for a happier past parallel to Wall Street's short-lived enthusiasm following Nixon's Proclamation of Emergency. It cited the jubilant bounces the stock market enjoyed, first in 1933 when President Roosevelt made his activist presence felt, and again in 1934 when he took the United States as far off gold as he had to in order to get American prices up, in the hope that employment would follow.

In one obvious respect the parallel is unmistakable. For Roosevelt then, as for Nixon now, the demand was less for specific actions than it was for any alternative to inaction. Merely meeting that demand was bound to act as a quick stimulant. "Doing something" was enough to bull the market for the moment. But the need "to do something else" quickly turned each rally into a selling opportunity.

The timing of each memorable Presidential proclamation explains the failure of Roosevelt's "devaluation bull market" to serve as a trustworthy guide for any presumption of a parallel Nixon bull market. Roosevelt's emergency moves effectively marked the end of the financial crisis of the 1930s. Nixon's merely formalized the arrival of the financial crisis of the 1970s. And, while Roosevelt's anti-depression actions were self-liquidating, Nixon's signaled the need for controls to continue into the indefinite future.

Even before the August 15 freeze made the de facto ceiling on dividends official, the uncompetitive yields on stock had made the stock market suspect. In a column I published at that time I pointed to the dividend-cutting action of U. S. Steel which had immediately put the stock market down. The arithmetic involved in U. S. Steel's action, and in the reaction of the stock market, suggested a future decline far sharper than had my own moderate projections. With the Dow Jones Industrial Average bouncing around 900, good seasoned workhorse stocks were yielding around 3 percent. Even then, with good bonds yielding twice as much, stock prices could not be expected to hold.

I caught more than my normal degree of thunder when I projected a 500 level for the Dow. And be clear, not projected as a low; projected as a test. I developed this projection on a twin premise: first, that cyclical fluctuations in the prices of stocks tend to gravitate to the level indicated by the dividends they pay; and, then, that investors were in the process of making a secular turn from trafficking in capital gains to investing in income.

Theoretically, dividend yields can rise for two reasons —either because dividend payments rise or, alternatively, because the prices investors pay to buy the same, or lower, dividends fall. My original projection of 500 as the decisive test level ahead for the Dow had preceded the President's Proclamation of Emergency. But it had rested on the same twin premise—that dividend payments were in a downward trend, and that income-mindedness would dominate the trend of stock prices. An increasingly glaring structural weakness in the stock market measures the rise of income-mindedness. The shrinkage of individual (as contrasted with institutional) participation in the stock market explains it. The most perplexing paradox in recent Wall Street history has been staged by the spectacle of professional investment ardor undampened by the realization that the "country cousins" have no immediate intention of buying a new stack of chips.

The money-using people in this country not only have dollars, they have sense. Having once decided that the stock market was more for gamblers than investors, they concluded that the turf there was too fast for them, and the payback there both too skimpy and too risky. The closest-read pages in every serious publication in this country today are the pocketbook pages. Although the country's editors have been slow to catch up with their readers' priorities, the flight of amateur investors from the high risks and low returns offered by the stock market has raised the risk and lowered the return on staying in it.

Why have they been leaving? Because they've wanted the same deal for their dollars that Meany's plumbers want for their time. They want to be paid, and rate of return is the measure. When market confidence returns, its leaders will not be glamour stocks. The leaders of the next bull market are going to be the workhorse, so-called income stocks which, at that point, pass muster not only because yields will be high but, even more importantly, because payoffs will be up. The major oil stocks may not be able to pass muster—as the relatively high yields they are already paying in a low-yield market suggest. Loss of their low-cost, Middle Eastern reserves would disqualify them for consideration. The utility stocks, like the bank stocks, qualify as the prime vehicles for prudent income-minded investment—when the price is right, the dividend income is adequate and competitive bond yields are falling.

But why 500? That was not a number I picked out of the air. I arrived at it in a very simple, conservative, moderate way. With net Treasury and Treasury-guaranteed borrowings approaching $40 billion a year—without consideration for the further squeeze that is still disturbing the economy, and that will deflate revenues and inflate borrowings—it is my judgment that 8 percent is a minimum floor under long-term bond yields.

Two subsidiary judgments reinforced this calculation. The first was provided by the behavior of the investing public. It had literally refinanced the country by absorbing the avalanche of bonds offered during the credit crunch at yields above 8 percent. But it simply stopped buying bonds when yields dropped below 8 percent. The second noted that the borrowings of the "debudgeted" agencies put greater pressure on the long-term bond market than on the shorter-term Treasury bill market. The government was relying on its ability to subsidize a housing start level of 2½ million units to maintain the illusion of prosperity. That level of housing starts in turn required a level of borrowing by the government-underwritten housing agencies sufficient to send the long-term bond market gravitating back to an 8 percent yield level.

The next step in the calculation invoked the 2 percent rule. This is simply stated. It takes two points to move money from one investment medium to another: a two-point spread always does. Eight percent for bonds, dictated as a floor by the bankrupt condition of the federal government, suggests a minimum 6 percent dividend level for stocks to keep money moving into stocks and out of bonds.

At this point, the calculation about bond yields relative to inflation, and the rule about the spread between interest and dividend yields, wants to be correlated with an older rule about the returns to be expected on good stocks. Over the years, good stocks of established companies producing basic products have gravitated to price levels at which their dividends have returned a trustworthy 5 percent cash yield. This 5 percent rule-of-thumb for the cash dividend yield on good stocks was confirmed during the years when money was sound and, therefore, cheaper to borrow than it is today. Now that lenders are demanding not only a return on their money, but a cost of inflation adjustment on top of it, the higher cost of money is calling for an upward adjustment in the cash return investors can be expected to demand from dividends before buying stocks again.

It is, thus, realistic to assume that a 6 percent dividend yield basis for stocks will be required to bring the public back into the stock market. A 6 percent return is also needed to satisfy pension fund fiduciaries under their heavier schedule of obligations foreshadowed by the last GM settlement. But in November 1971, Dow Industrials were yielding under 4 percent, paying somewhat more than $30.00 as an aggregate dividend and selling at 900. To yield 6 percent, assuming the decline in dividends does not breach the $30.00 level, the Dow Jones Industrial Average would have to fall to 500.

Another way of quantifying the same calculation is to project a yield basis for Dow-grade Industrials equal to the actual 1971–72 yield basis for Telephone, which was 6 percent—and with no buying enthusiasm stirred up by it.

So the number 500, while it seems to be chilling, is actually a projection which I developed before it became apparent that dividends were not going to rise, and while the market was not yet reconciled to the reality that they were going to be cut. And lest there be any doubt as to the moderation of this projection, let's take a look at U. S. Steel and ALCOA.

The great post-depression bull market can be regarded as dating from U. S. Steel's ability to resume dividend payments. As for ALCOA, it was the greatest growth stock on the Board when the market and the economy it reflected were strongest and soundest. By the eve of 1971's post-Thanksgiving rally, these prime media for America's basic production strength had already suffered a 75 percent deflation in price, with the test still ahead.

Their intensive bear markets had been discounted on the theory that we have evolved from an economy of goods into an economy of services. It is my judgment that, if we don't re-evolve into an economy of goods, we're in worse trouble than even I think.

The case of the glamour stocks further sharpens my calculation. Every one of the nation's great growth stocks happens to represent a multinational company. And they were all caught in the overseas meat grinder. The rape which has been perpetrated on America's primary industries by our government inside the American market is now going to be duplicated on our multinational corporations by the governments which were our clients, became our competitors, and are now our creditors. In the next phase of market break, these multinational glamour stocks are going to get the treatment which America's primary industries have already received.

Given my major premise of a fundamental switch from chasing capital gains to income-mindedness on the part of the investing public, the multinational stocks—or yesterday's "glamour girls"—would be vulnerable by virtue of the fact that their going yields are little more than half the yields paid by the stocks comprising the Dow Jones Industrial Average. "Aunt Jane's favorites" of the last generation is the way to think of the Dow stocks. If you were to project the 75 percent deflation which U.S. Steel and ALCOA had suffered by 1971 for the Dow as a whole, you would be projecting a bottom not of 500 but of 250. And I am not projecting 250. I am simply explaining how moderate is my own projection of the test at 500—a testing of a 6 percent dividend yield basis for the Dow stocks.

While America's multinational companies are in trouble up to their corporate ears overseas, safety is the traditional hallmark of her public utility corporations. They are the one class of business entitled by law to earn minimal rates of return on their investment. This represents not merely a trade-off because their profits are regulated. It also guarantees them the ability to raise the money they need in order to provide the facilities that the public wants for the utility services it uses. A second regulatory trade-off explains the premium quality status enjoyed by utility dividends: the safety of their flow plus the safety of the bet on them to be increased steadily, if gradually.

Utility stocks are preeminently money stocks. Their market movements, therefore, serve as symptomatic early warnings of the influence of money conditions on stock prices. A drop in interest rates invariably triggers a rally in utility stock prices; and, moreover, establishes the leadership role of utility stock prices for the market as a whole while interest rates continue downward. So long as 1971 market expectations speculated on lower interest rates, higher utility stock prices led the market. The moment the budget deficit bombshell blasted the illusion, utility stock prices turned down before interest rates turned up. Symptomatically, the Dow Utility average continued to fall during 1972 despite reassuring predictions of lower interest rates packaged with the official announcement of lower government deficits.

Even more fundamentally, the lackluster performance of utility stocks in late 1971 reflected the market's reluctance to take high utility dividend payouts at face value. And with good reason. The reliability of utility dividends got caught in the cruel squeeze between the hard line taken by the Price Commission and the soft line taken by the Pay Board. The Pay Board abdicated its authority to approve all wage-rate increases in favor of the Construction Industry Stabilization Committee, which proceeded to approve the big inflationary wage hikes that had been responsible for bringing on the emergency officially proclaimed on August 15. But the Price Commission was banning all applications for rate increases; and the Price Commission had assumed control over the right of the state regulatory commission to approve utility rate increases. Little wonder that the market was regarding the rich dividend yields of utilities—up to and above 7 percent —as too good to be true.

Additional perspective on the risks built into the stock market as it was bulled is suggested by the provocative practices of the country's pension funds, including some of the largest and most respectable of them. The invitation they have offered to a regulatory crackdown is summarized in Chapter 5 on Personal Finances. Marketwise, however, the threat they offer recalls a major lesson of speculative and regulatory history. The time lag between speculative excess and regulatory catchup is built into the interactions between the speculative cycle and the regulatory process. Not until after an overbulled stock market has first created its own excesses and then destroyed itself are regulatory restraints brought into play to prevent a repeat performance.

Meanwhile, the sequence of investigation and crackdown has the effect of taking the surprise out of any new bust, while guaranteeing that the next boom will start as a surprise. The climactic blowoff rally of 1971–72 started *after* the mutual funds had suffered a crippling loss of liquidity. It was paced by the speculative excesses of pension funds insensitive to the collision course they were traveling with new regulatory crackdowns. Thus, the pension funds multiplied the vulnerability of the "institutional" market they dominated to the crackdown they provoked.

The more than incidental circumstance that a disturbing number of pension fund managements have found themselves unfunded, relative to their accrued obligations to tomorrow's retirees, explains their scramble to play "the gains game." For example, in late 1971 the pension plan of a major aerospace company had approximately $349,000,000 in liabilities for accrued vested benefits, although the market value of its assets was only $273,-000,000. If the pension plan had terminated at that time, employees with vested benefits would have had no legal remedy to obtain all their vested benefits. This illustration not only points up the risk of betting on the stock market to put missing cash back in the till; it also emphasizes the need for a regulatory crackdown on pension fund speculation in the stock market.

A footnote is in order on the oddball breed of securities known as warrants. Warrants are options. They are options to buy stock under explicit conditions as to time and price set forth in the terms of warrant itself. For example, holders of a particular warrant may put up a dollar today for the privilege of having the option to buy stock at $10.00 a share within the next five years. If the stock is selling in the market for $20.00 a share, of course they will exercise their option. By the same token, a warrant carrying this right is certain to sell at a high price in the market—because of the $10.00 difference between the current price of the stock and the exercise price of the warrant, and possibly an additional premium that reflects the chance that the stock's price may rise further before the warrant expires. Contrariwise, when a warrant carries the right to buy a share of stock at $10.00 and the stock is selling at only $5.00 in the market, the warrant holder will not find it worthwhile to exercise the option. The warrant will still have a market value, again because of the possibility that it may become profitable to exercise it before the warrant expires.

Warrants are generally given as a bonus incentive to buyers of new issues of debentures. They represent a "kicker"—not so much a piece of the action as the privilege of participating in the action if and when there is any. The terms of any warrant vary with the deal. Warrants can be offered in perpetuity or they may expire in a relatively short period. A middle way is to phase out previous offerings by scaling up the exercise price over a period of years.

Warrants are very speculative instruments; and, when they promise to carry a valuable exercise privilege of conversion, they generally command premium prices. They do not participate in the dividend privileges of the stocks into which they are convertible.

Investment advisers earn their keep when they can evaluate the comparative advantages of warrants. Big plays in warrants assume good plays in the stocks underlying them. But all warrants are speculative—even the warrants of American Telephone and Telegraph. The warrant itself carries no ownership in the equity of the company. It is a call or option on the warrant-holder's right to buy equity—if and when the warrant privilege is exercised.

Q: How do you rate the old-line blue chips versus the glamour stocks?

Mr. C. C. B. (Oakland, California)

A: The demoralization that has hit the stock market is separating the men from the boys. The boys are turning their backs on the stock fashions of their own creation. The men are starting to take a hard look at the bargains beginning to turn up in the securities of companies which have not only a past but a future and which, more than incidentally, have enough money in the bank to tide them over in the present.

As recently as spring 1969, while the market swingers were still exploiting the fashion show, they were sneering at how square it was to be interested in old-line blue chips like General Motors. A remark by one of the most flamboyant characters satirized in Adam Smith's *Money Game* caught the spirit of that era: "General Motors is a stock to have inherited, not to buy."

But suddenly the old rules have replaced the new. Yesterday's stock spectaculars, which were held together by twigs, have fallen apart for lack of the glue that only liquidity can provide when money is right. The stocks that young fund managers had priced out of sight are going bidless.

By the same token, the stocks of the big companies, which were "out" while money seemed unimportant, are becoming "in" again now that stocks with money behind them are again commanding a bigger premium than stocks with stories presumed to be in front of them.

Q: I am thirty-one years old, married and a secretary. My nest egg is 25 shares of IBM. Our only debt is the 5 percent mortgage on our home. My husband recently up-dated our life insurance to $60,000. My husband feels that computer stocks no longer have the growth potential they enjoyed in the past, and wants me to sell 16 shares and buy something less vulnerable. What do you suggest?

Mrs. P. K. (Clarendon Hills, Illinois)

A: Your husband is right about the computer stocks having lost their growth potential. My own judgment is that, instead of being merely overpriced and yielding an unacceptably low income, they are caught in a new bear market of their own—thanks to their critical dependence on overseas earnings, which are eroding as a direct consequence of the continuing international monetary mess.

When computer stocks were the big glamour stocks, they went up twice as fast as the Dow average during up-ward moves. I expect this two-to-one ratio to apply on the downside—meaning the stocks will go down twice as fast.

While I agree with your husband's general judgment, I am worried that his suggested selling strategy may be cutting things too fine for people in your position. The big question for you seems to be the simple one of "in or out," not running the risk of trying to squeeze something extra out of your nest egg. You'd be better off selling out altogether. Your peace of mind about your security is worth more than trying for the top dollar.

Q: Why do brokers, consultants and financial advisers fail to point out that many utility companies offer federal income tax advantages on their dividends?

Mr. E. G. (Bloomington, Minnesota)

A: "Have been" would be more accurate. Noting that the country's utilities have paid out some $260 million in annual tax-free dividends, Congress has just about ended this privilege, beginning in 1973. The tax-sheltered utility dividend privilege was due to utilities taking fast depreciation on their heavy plant investments. But even without this privilege, utility dividend yields are now becoming attractively high—granted that they are measuring present risks more than future opportunities.

Q: Do you think there is any chance that AT&T will reduce its dividends in the near future when the market goes down, as you predict? The company never has in the past, but I am very pessimistic about the future.

Mrs. S. A. (Forest Hills, New York)

A: Don't overdo your pessimism or project it too far into the future. Difficult though the present is, the Telephone dividend is every bit as trustworthy as your sense of caution.

By way of perspective on the controversy that was stirred up by my warning that the Dow Jones Industrial stocks were in for a test at the 500 level, utility stocks are already selling on an equivalent basis. Their performance suggests that they are in for a further drop that will send their dividend yields still higher.

Q: I have $25,000 in utility and insurance stocks; $30,000 in certificates of deposit; and $25,000 in long-term utility bonds yielding from 7.5 to 8 percent. In view of the market's recent performance and forecasts for more hard times, would you suggest a change in my investment plan?

Mr. R. P. (Saginaw, Michigan)

A: You will do better to pay less attention to buying "chances" on the market and more to clarifying your own purposes and supporting program. Spreading $25,000 between utility and insurance stocks, as you are doing, will give you the benefit accruing from neither of these prime long-term equity vehicles.

Insurance stocks offer low yields and utility stocks high yields. Make up your mind which group has the economic claim on priority for your purposes. The highest yields consistent with the lowest risks would better suit your needs.

With the higher yielding group of utility stocks yielding 6½ to 7½ percent in a 7½ percent bond market, utility stocks are now more attractive than utility bonds. The decline in utility stocks, at a time when utility bonds have been trying to rally, will keep them more attractive until the next time utility bonds yield at least 2 percent more than utility stocks. You would do well to switch your utility bonds as well as your insurance stocks into utility stocks. This will serve to increase your investment income and will enable you to add to your capital over the longer term.

Q: You have said that life insurance stocks won't regain their highs of a few years ago until there is a return to lower interest rates. But life insurance companies are lenders of money and not borrowers. It seems to me that they should benefit from the higher interest rates. The same argument would apply to bank stocks. Where is my reasoning wrong?

Mr. C. F. (East Aurora, New York)

A: It's too simplistic. "Money stocks"—banks, Savings and Loans, insurance companies, finance companies—rise when the price of the commodity they have to sell falls. Why should this be any more confusing than that Henry Ford bought profitable volume when he cut his prices?

The recurrent credit crunches caused by the inflationary crisis have left insurance companies vulnerable to one conspicuously unprofitable obligation: to make low-rate loans to policyholders, even to the point of having to pay high rates themselves when they are overcommitted in order to make good on this obligation. Another difficulty in the way of insurance stocks during an inflationary spiral reflects their position as long-term lenders. Massive portions of their portfolios were committed at long-term.

True, when investment conditions tightened up, they were able to renegotiate many loans at higher rates. Nevertheless, their investment yields are subject to time lags. But perhaps the most pragmatic argument against accumulating insurance stocks during an inflationary squeeze reflects their strength rather than their weakness. They are far and away the best and the most dynamic of the financial stocks. The buyers they attract are sophisticated, upper-bracket individuals. Insurance stocks are "rich men's stocks." But this is the very class of investor most likely to seek sanctuary in Treasury bills or short-term municipals when inflationary pressures are squeezing investor confidence. After all, it takes buyers to bid stocks up.

Bank stocks are more cyclically sensitive to money conditions than are insurance stocks. Suburban and country bank stocks are prime growth vehicles for on-the-spot investors in a position not to be troubled by their lack of ready marketability.

Q: Several years ago, I bought a small amount of insurance stock which is now worth about $70,000. The company, twenty years old, has an excellent growth record, and pays a 5 percent dividend annually. Do you think such stock will drop in the months ahead? Would I be wise to sell some of my holdings now and pay the gain tax?

Mrs. R. C. (Almira, Washington)

A: I do, but anyone getting a 5 percent yield on the original cost of a good insurance stock would have to pay a whopping capital gain tax if the entire holding were liquidated. Your cost seems low enough to give you a cushion against any decline in prospect. Why don't you consider selling enough shares to recoup your original investment? This will minimize your gain tax liability and it will leave you in the position of riding for free. Meanwhile, 5 percent on quality insurance stocks doesn't grow on apple trees.

Q: My wife and I are both seventy years of age and have an income of $300 a month from Social Security, and approximately $100 a month from dividends and savings accounts. Our investments include utility and oil stocks, and I am wondering whether to take $4,000 out of our savings account to invest in more good yielding income stocks. I am worried, however, that I might speculate wrongly. I must increase my income to help pay our property taxes of $762 a year which, with inflation what it is, have become a big burden. This is our only problem since we own our home, and have adequate health and life insurance. I would very much appreciate your advice on whether my plan would be taking too much of a gamble with our capital.

Mr. B. J. (Wethersfield, Connecticut)

A: All oil companies are subject to too many tax and regulatory hazards to make sense for people in their seventies who need income and who have no chance of replacing capital losses. Choosing between utility stocks and bonds is your best bet. With utility stock yields close to utility bond yields, an argument in favor of bonds for people in your circumstances is that the interest they pay is calculated by the day. This means that if you need to raise money for an emergency, you will get your rate of return. If you sell a stock between dividend dates, you lose your current dividend. Remember that your property taxes are a deduction against any taxable income you receive.

Q: Do you think that a complete or partial cutoff of Middle Eastern oil is possible? If so, how seriously would this affect international oil stocks? Also, are foreign economic and political difficulties amply discounted in the current prices of oil shares? I own an international oil stock and, although I am just about even, I am worried.

Mr. F. J. S. (Northbrook, Illinois)

A: My best judgment is that no market adjustment could amply discount the political dangers overhanging traditional oil values in the Middle East. Between Arab nationalism and Soviet imperialism, the international oil companies are going to be under endless pressure to raise immeasurable sums of new high-cost capital to replace their low-cost Middle Eastern reserves. And the stocks of companies in need of new money invariably come under selling pressure.

While there have been recurrent short-term plays in the international oils, I think that the longer-term risks outweigh the incentives to take this chance. Why not take advantage of any speculative run-up to get out of your international oil into a quality domestic oil? The market in American oil shares is benefiting from the troubles plaguing the international oils; and it will continue to do so.

Q: I am the thirty-two-year-old father of two sons, aged six and four. My wife and I are trying to accumulate education funds for them. During the last eighteen months, we have purchased a few hundred shares of oil shale stock, which we feel will be of value in ten to twelve years.

Mr. I. D. (Portland, Oregon)

A: There is no doubt whatever that America's rich shale-oil reserves represent a major source of growth earning power for the future. But the economic way to invest in this growth potential is through the securities of major oil companies with a headstart in this field, not by taking fliers on the speculative stocks of smaller companies lacking the needed capital.

The shale-minded investor who makes his play on the future in major oil company securities will be well paid for waiting, but it will be a very expensive game to get into. It's not for small players or for quick fliers.

Q: I am past three score and ten, and work only a few hours a day in my office. My wife and I are in good health and our sons are married. My assets, accumulated over a period of time, include $550,000 in tax-free bonds; some 3,600 shares of stock in oil, gas, paper, sulphur, and glass; 15,700 shares of mutual funds; and $147,000 in U.S. bonds. What would you suggest for further investment?

Mr. C. H. (Winnetka, Illinois)

A: I half agree with what you have been doing—specifically, with your prudence in limiting your tax-free portion to short-term maturities falling due before 1975. But I believe that you have also stayed too long with too much in your oil, gas, paper, sulphur, and glass stocks. Your life expectancy doesn't allow for much long-term capital accumulation from these stock holdings. But it does expose you to the risk of losing a significant portion of what you have accumulated. If this happens, you will use up time increasingly precious to you waiting until your stock holdings recover. Selling enough of your shares to recoup your original investment would mini-

mize the capital gains tax you would have to pay on the
cheap stock you bought early in your investment career
and leave you free to ride on your profits. You could put
the proceeds of your bailout into more short-term, tax-
free income.

*Q: I am one of the Gulf Gold Coast's younger retirees,
in my early fifties, and up to this point I have done well
putting my spare investment cash into the good securities
of companies in industries of which I have had professional knowledge at first hand. I was a power company
engineer in West Virginia and Virginia and, because of
my observation of the coal shortage in America's best coal
fields, I have been a systematic buyer of the best coal
stocks on every market reaction.*

*While I agree with your often quoted adage that
"they"—they meaning the government—"can't print
land," I think it is just as true that no one is finding good
new coal deposits where American industry needs them.
Just because my theory and my practice have worked out
so well for me so far, I am anxious to have your slant on
any risks I may be overlooking.*

Mr. E. V. E. (St. Petersburg, Florida)

A: As a matter of business economics, your reasoning
and your observations were right as rain—until only yesterday. The shrinkage in the world market has made the
difference. While it was still expanding, the American
coal producers were able to ride a sellers' market. I suspect that they may have been making too much of a good
thing when the world boom was still at its crest. Now
that shrinkage is the trend, they are exposed to strong

price competition from the rich Australian coal fields. Political pressures are also suggesting that the party is over for coal stocks. Nowadays, any time any business benefits from a price boom, it risks running into a political buzz saw. The runaway in fuel prices has become vulnerable to Washington crackdowns and arm-twistings. Coal stocks are now subject to both pricing and political troubles.

Q: I am in a quandary over what to do with my $50,000 in Treasury bonds and 700 shares of steel stock. I am seventy-two, a widow with no dependents. I do not play the market and am only interested in a steady income. I bought my steel stock thirty years ago and I hesitate to take such a loss should I sell now. What do you advise?

Mrs. H. R. (Fort Lauderdale, Florida)

A: Take your loss now before you lose your dividend income from it as well. As to your $50,000 in Treasury bonds, you will increase your income by switching them into corporates or utilities which are of better quality.

Q: I am an attorney, age twenty-five, with an annual income of $12,000. I have $5,200 in a Savings and Loan account; 25 shares of AT&T; one convertible bond; and some 275 shares in three industrials—for a total of $18,000. I soon hope to be saving $400 a month. Would you consider steel for long-term investment?

Mr. W. S. (Riverside, Illinois)

A: No—even after the market bottoms out. In fact, not until America recovers her competitive position in her own backyard and internationally as well. Then, and only then, will steel be a market leader again.

Meanwhile, your best bet is not to try to outguess this tricky market, but to build all the buying power you can in order to have the wherewithal to pick up bargains when the time comes. And it's not right around the corner either.

As you build up your professional income, you'll accumulate more capital buying short-term tax-exempts, banking the interest and playing the stock market carefully.

Q: My husband and I bought silver mining stocks at twice the price of what they sell for now and kept buying on the way down. Now we have 18,000 shares and, since their price must be at or near rock-bottom, we are tempted to buy more.

Would we be asking for more trouble, or are silver prices due to make a comeback?

Mrs. M. A. H. (New Port Richey, Florida)

A: "Must" is a word investors never use. Speculators use it at their peril.

Silver has certainly been overdue for some sort of rally. The dollar devaluation rally in the stock market helped it to one in the wake of the gold speculation. But no silver recovery can expect a long life expectancy. Too much of an overhang in speculative hands is waiting to sandbag it with selling pressures. Your speculation would be more realistic if you'd been playing the silver market itself. You will be asking for trouble so long as you own anything like your present block of silver shares—even if they are in the penny-and-dollar class. You are way overcommitted in this crap game.

Q: An investment adviser stated the other day that "both gold and silver shares offer an opportunity of a lifetime." Do you agree with him? He supports your forecast of 500 on the Dow.

Mr. C. K. (*Hickory Hills, Illinois*)

A: I may be proven right about the stock market even though he agrees with me about it.

Q: We are in our early forties and have three young children. We became interested in atomic power nine years ago and bought some uranium stock. Watching the continued growth of atomic power has been a hobby with us—one that we hesitate to give up. But we could do so if it seemed advisable to pay off our mortgage. What would you do?

Mr. R. W. M. (*Nappance, Indiana*)

A: Quality investment in the long-term growth of uranium and nuclear power values represents a more economic use of funds than freezing cash in mortgage repayment. But this may not be saying much. Nuclear power is a prime target of the anti-pollution crusade.

Q: I recall hearing you speak in the 1950s when you were very bullish on the economy and the stock market in general, and on railroad stocks in particular. Would you still be bullish on railroad stocks if you could see a genuine follow-through in economic recovery?

Mr. G. M. D. (*Columbus, Ohio*)

A: Yes, I would, and for the reason you suggest. Good railroad stocks are plays par excellence on volume. Their relatively small capitalizations, plus the leverage built into their debt, invariably sends them flying when volume rises. True, they are vulnerable to aggressive break-throughs in labor costs, as well as to onerously impractical regulation. To take just one example of this jeopardy, enormous savings from dieselization never reached the stockholder because they were diverted to pick up the tab for wage increases and featherbedding. Nevertheless, taking into account every conceivable warning that has been uttered against the railroads as wards of the regulatory authorities, I think that they will pay their way any time high volume sets the stage for a stock market follow-through to higher levels. One way of looking at the railroads is as the small private speculator's equivalent of the high capitalization, high-price growth stocks.

Reference to the basic principle that the prices of stocks rise with their dividend-paying power puts the question about railroad stocks in the larger perspective of the entirely public sector/private sector relationship. Transportation has admittedly been caught in the collision between the two—but not irretrievably. Next time the practicalities prevail in the public sector, and the traffic tangle between the public sector and the private sector is set right, the railroads will be freed and required to raise new capital. A return of their dividend-paying power will be a condition of it. Recovery by their stocks will give the signal for it.

One warning: rail stocks were going out of fashion as the stock market was taking on its institutional character. The rails have never been institutional favorites. The institutional fraternity prefers the airline stocks, which are even more leverage-loaded than the rails because of their greater and continuous need for more debt. They also have the larger capitalizations appropriate for use by the institutional investor. This means that moves in rail stocks are dependent on the willingness and ability of the large private speculator to anticipate big moves. Nevertheless, I believe that the next sound bull market will see a healthy switch in government attitude toward the railroads and that the rails will participate in the next bull market. Liking them still seems to me to be a condition of liking the market.

Q: Aerospace stocks have been falling steadily. All of these companies have introduced new products that should increase their sales volume, and indicate strength instead of weakness, even in a bear market. How come they're going down?

Mr. R. F. C. (Seattle, Washington)

A: The inflationary cost squeeze has raised risks and costs for establishing new products. It has lengthened the time needed to get a payback on them and lowered the rate of return. This goes double for the advanced technology field, for two reasons: it is capital-intensive, which makes financing unprofitable; and government is the major customer, which makes profit unlikely. The airlines are the other customer; and, in their strained condition, this makes for slim sales pickings. The coming resurgence in U. S. arms spending is not likely to start a bull market in aerospace stocks. It is more likely to provoke an irresistible demand for stringent profit ceilings on the industry.

Q: Would the major commercial airline stocks be a good buy for capital appreciation over the next five years or so?

Mr. E. B. E. (Cleveland, Ohio)

A: I doubt it—even though airline management has done a tremendous job, under difficult conditions, of controlling its costs and limiting its commitments.

Airline stocks are the first to go up on bear market rallies and the most vulnerable to subsequent corrections. Their winter take-off signaled the start of 1971's year-end rally; and their spring setback signaled its comeuppance. The whole transportation sector of the market is subject to the cost squeeze in general, to capital-raising problems in particular, and to the blight of regulation.

Q: I own $60,000 of a major broadcasting company common and preferred stock, on which I owe $33,000. The dividends just about equal the interest I pay on my collateral loan. I am fifty-two, and am interested in building an early retirement fund. Do you advise selling the stock, paying off the loan, and reinvesting the balance of about $20,000 in better paying stock, bonds, or certificates of deposit? If the market goes down, as you predict, I'd be on a better footing if I had cash in the bank.

Mr. J. H. (Glencoe, Illinois)

A: You have answered your own question. I fear that the well-known troubles that come with getting priced out of markets could hurt even the best broadcasting stock. They have been suffering since the onset of the profit squeeze as the result of the advertising switch from brand to price advertising. The bloom is off the rose so far as the broadcast business is concerned. For the last several years, it has been the most profitable single industry in the country. Now even it has been laying off people.

More fundamentally, however, regardless of whether the stock on which you owe money happens to represent an investment in broadcasting or any other industry, I think this is a dangerous time to be carrying stock on margin, whether in the bank or with brokers.

Q: In view of the breathtaking increases in health costs, and the fact that both the government and corporation pension funds are putting up so much money to foot the bills, why aren't nursing home stocks a good buy?

Mr. A. M. (New York, N. Y.)

A: Your observation is realistic but your reasoning is not. It runs smack into the rule that companies whose business is great need even more cash than companies whose business is punk. All the nursing home stocks have speculative allure because the demand for commercial health services is rising faster than anyone can count. But don't expect the stock of any company needing new money in a sick capital market to act healthy. Growth and demand do not guarantee investment appreciation.

Q: Do you think that pharmaceutical stocks are a good investment now?

Mrs. D. B. (Omaha, Nebraska)

A: The more profitable a pharmaceutical company is today, the more vulnerable its price structure and public relations are to regulatory crackdowns. Also, the most dynamic American pharmaceutical companies are most dependent on foreign investment and foreign borrowing and, therefore, are most vulnerable to shrinkage in the world economy. The danger of retaliatory crackdowns against the foreign subsidiaries of American corporations is not to be minimized either. I'd hold off.

Q: I often see you recommending property as an investment. Do you think property stocks are a good buy as well?

Mr. A. B. L. (Hartford, Connecticut)

A: Theoretically, they would be the very best. The practical pitfalls, however, are just as obvious as the theoretical attractions.

Securities buyable as property stocks fall into two groups: those of companies in other lines of work which happen to have rich property holdings, and those of land development companies.

The most obvious and tempting example of property-rich asset values deemed to be going at deep discounts is offered by the railroads. But while western railroads in particular own empires of undeveloped acreage unreflected in their market prices and offering enormous potential for future development, unfortunately none of them have the managerial "oomph" to maximize this second string to their bow.

The land development companies may have aggressive and imaginative management, but they are still vulnerable to inflationary squeezes on the credit and labor markets. The high cost of construction puts high hurdles in the way of converting land from its raw state into profitable

use. And once this income-producing construction is put
in place, it generally has to be sold on the installment plan,
subject to small down payments, resulting in long lead-
times between investment and payback. And development
companies, while rich in paper earnings, are short of cash.

By investing in property stocks you run up against the
kind of risks I recommend avoiding by buying property
itself. But one of these days a management in the property business will develop the investment answer to avoid
these risks. Meanwhile, the big new development in the
funds game centers on the setting up of funds that enable investors to buy participation in property assets in the
form of fund shares. This idea is already well established
in Britain.

*Q: My wife and I are both in our early thirties. We
have a young family and each of us has a good job. Both
of us have inherited enough capital to free us to distin-
guish between income needs for the present and investment targets for the future.*

*Our plan is to put our inheritances to work for us while
we live on our current earnings. Of the investment standards you repeatedly refer to in your newspaper column,
timing is not important to us but selectivity is. Where do
you think patient investors like us will do well to look for
the next generation of stock market leaders?*

Mr. R. G. (Great Neck, Long Island)

A: For the time being, your question is easier to answer in industry terms than in specific company terms.
Building is the most likely candidate for stock market
leadership the next time investor confidence returns.

A favorable investment climate is also likely to shift the relationship of leaders to laggards inside the stock market. Inflation has been benefiting the industries rendering services more than the industries delivering hard goods. But I think that the next bull market, when it finally starts, will swing the leadership role back to the securities of companies producing hard, tangible goods.

The reason the building industry is a place to look is simple. Whereas the markets for many hard goods are saturated, unsubsidized quality housing is in short supply.

But identifying building as the next market leadership group is easier to do today than identifying the particular companies in the field most likely to lead the group when its day comes. Before financing and labor costs were inflated, the leading residential construction stocks were suppliers of building materials. I believe that inflationary financing requirements are subordinating the traditional workhorse role of the old-time speculative builder of homes or apartment houses.

I suspect that the next crop of building industry leaders will come not from the materials producers serving the builders and the contractors but, rather, from the emergent group of city developers affiliated with financial institutions. Before that day comes, however, recognition that subsidized housing has been hopelessly overbuilt is bound to put all building securities on the bargain counter.

$
$
CHAPTER – – $ – – **11**
$
$
$ **BONDS**
$
$
$

The bond market always seems to be the most obvious of investment media—partly because the terms of investment are fixed. Nevertheless, the bond market has always been, and remains more than ever, the most professional of investment media—more so than the stock market. It is also a bigger market.

America owes a vast debt to her growing corps of bond buyers. They saved her from a panic during the 1970 credit crunch. The rich yields that were offered then for a record volume of offerings found small takers on a large scale. It is no exaggeration to say that the money which income-minded investors put into bonds all through that credit siege saved not only the bond market but the country. In the process, it enlarged the orbit of the bond market in time to prevent the borrowing scramble from reaching panic proportions.

Distress in the bond market signaled the onset of the last great depression. Contrariwise, recovery in the bond market—as measured by the dramatic return to lower interest rates—subsequently signaled the return of recovery to the stock market and to the economy behind it.

The stock market and the bond market travel together

—even though prosperity for the bond market assumes some measure of setback for corporate earnings and business activity and, therefore, for the stock market. Since 1968 the stock market has been subject to erratic, wide-swinging pressures, with the burden on it to prove that it is not in the early stages of a major new bear market. But in the last few years the bond market has been suffering a private 1929 of its own. As it has fallen, it has attracted a new consensus among the silent majority whose members are steadily casting their pocketbook votes on the side of bonds. Inveterate savers and former stock-chasers alike have been putting their four- and five-figure accumulations into this income-getting paper whenever the yield has justified the commitment.

A simple rule, measurable with two thumbs and one finger, illustrates the way the bond market has been working and can be counted on to continue working for the duration of the present inflationary crisis. Regardless of the rate of earnings, regardless of the rate of taxation, and regardless of the rate of inflation, experience suggests that money is worth a constant return of 3 percent. If, therefore, a 5 percent rate of inflation is anticipated in any given year, those minded to invest in bonds will hold out for the normal 3 percent rate of return—plus the 5 percent cost adjustment for the rate of inflation, or 8 percent. The difference between the going rate of return on long-term bonds and the 3 percent constant rate of return on money measures expectations as to the current rate of inflation.

Reflecting this rule of 3 percent as the constant return required by money, plus an add-on to compensate for the cost of inflation, bonds will need to yield a minimum of 8 percent in order to attract genuine investor interest. Any time they yield more, investors show themselves willing and, indeed, anxious to gobble them up. Any time they yield less, speculation takes over. The recurrent rallies of the bond market find professional dealers alternately tempted and obligated to warehouse large market overhangs, in the hope that the public will decide that the inflationary siege has been lifted; and that, therefore, it can afford to absorb bonds for investment at yields under 8 percent. But for the duration of the inflationary crisis, a bond market yielding less than 8 percent is guaranteed to lose its investment following. Professional speculation on turnover gains from markups measuring drops in the interest rate is a chancy and temporary substitute.

Up to this point, recurrent speculation on the part of the professional securities-dealing fraternity has been frustrated. I think that it will continue to be so—certainly so long as the federal government needs to raise upward of $50 billion a year to finance an admitted budget deficit of $30 billion, and, consequently, push up inflationary requirements for rates of return deemed high enough to provide insurance against inflation—that is, 8 percent.

A word is in order on the nature of bonds. Bonds are long-term obligations to pay a fixed number of dollars in interest each year, and a fixed number of dollars—the principal—back at the end of a specified time. The interest rate is based on the face value of the bond, generally $1,000, so that the amount of dollars paid during its life is almost always fixed in advance.

A bond that guarantees the payment of $50 per year in interest until it matures, for example, has what is termed a nominal interest rate of 5 percent. If it matures in twenty years, the holders of the bond during its life will have received $1,000 in interest payments by the time it matures, and will then receive the $1,000 of principal. If interest rates fall, bond issuers will want to redeem their outstanding bonds bearing high interest rates in order to borrow at lower cost. When interest rates are high, investors demand—and get—"call protection" against early redemption of new issues, often for five to ten years on twenty- to thirty-year bonds.

Bonds come in a variety of shapes from a variety of borrowers. Corporations—above all, public utilities—and state and local governments are the biggest issuers, because they make the biggest long-term capital investments. Understandably, because of the way our system works, today's state and local government bond issues are tomorrow's state and local taxes.

The federal government also issues bonds—when it can. It hasn't been able to do so—on the table, at least—for some years, because of a statutory ceiling on the interest rate the U. S. Treasury can pay on debt with a maturity of more than seven years. Many state and local governments also face interest ceilings, but their interest payments to investors are tax-free, unlike those of the Treasury and corporations. These ceilings have only restricted long-term municipal borrowings in the past two years.

Meantime, the various "alphabet agencies" of the federal government have managed to sell bonds on a wholesale basis. Their offerings are more or less guaranteed by the federal government. Not merely legal advice—but the legendary instinct for fine print of Philadelphia lawyers—is needed to ferret out the distinction between federal government agency bonds which are and are not guaranteed by the federal government; and, if so, whether as to interest and/or principal.

As a practical matter, it is probably pragmatic to go on the assumption that either all bonds issued by all federal agencies are as "money-good" as if they were Treasury bills or that none of them are. The rising risk which has been growing with the supply has been building an upward bias into the rate of return yielded by federal government agency bonds.

Bonds are issued not only to finance long-term capital investment. They are also issued in order to "fund" accumulated short-term borrowings. The demand for long-term money in the first half of 1970—that is, the backlog of bond issues ready to come to market—was made up in large part of borrowers who either could not legally borrow at recent market interest rates or who trusted their "expert" advice that interest rates would come down soon, and substantially. Despite a record volume of bond issues for the past year, short-term debts remained enormous and so did the need to issue bonds.

The market constantly adjusts the value of outstanding bonds to bring the nominal interest rate on outstanding bonds (the rate shown on the coupon) into line with the current rate on new issues. If interest rates go up, the prices of outstanding bonds will go down; and if interest rates go down, bond prices will go up. For example, if the interest rate on newly issued bonds is 10 percent, the market value of an old $1,000 bond paying 5 percent will adjust downward toward $500. The result will be that an investor, after the price adjustment, will be able to get the same $100 yield on a $1,000 investment either by buying one new bond yielding 10 percent at its face value or two old bonds yielding 5 percent at half their face value.

No matter how far the price of a bond falls during the course of its life—how deep a "discount" the market puts on a bond—at maturity the holder of the bond is entitled to its full face value. This leads to two different ways of calculating the value of the income received by the purchaser of a bond. The "current yield" is simply derived by dividing the annual interest payment by the current market price of the bond. The "yield to maturity" takes into account the capital gain—the difference between current price and face value—that purchasers will receive if they hold bonds until they mature, as well as the interest payments.

Bond investors paying more than par to get the going rate of return on lower coupons in a higher-rate market—for example, paying more than par to buy an 8 percent yield on a 7⅞ percent coupon—run the risk of absorbing a capital loss at maturity. Alternatively, if it suits their tax purposes, they can anticipate a capital loss on top of the high income they earn.

Because interest payments are still taxed at full rates as ordinary income, while capital gains accrued over a period of more than six months are taxed at substantially lower rates, "deep discount" bonds—most of whose yield to maturity is accounted for by capital gains—can be particularly attractive on an after-tax basis. If interest rates on new issues are likely to fall sharply, thus raising the market price on outstanding bonds and providing their holders with capital gains, deep discount bonds can be attractive even if the purchaser does not intend to hold them to maturity.

Just as a fall in interest rates and a rise in bond prices is a reliable leading indicator of a follow-through rise in stock prices, so a movement of sophisticated money to deep discount bonds—with a sensitive eye to the built-in capital gains they offer—is a sure-fire leading indicator of a rise in bond prices.

Deep discount bonds offer the first, the safest, and the biggest gains the moment any surge of high interest rates is broken. True, the stock market rises then, too. But the deep discount bond market leads the stock market. Moreover, for the professional player, borrowing on deep discount bonds yields more dynamic leverage than borrowing on stocks when and as interest rates drop.

Aside from "straight debt," described above, corporate borrowers can also issue "convertible debentures." Convertibles pay interest at a fixed rate on a fixed sum. But they also have an "equity kicker": at some specified future time they are convertible into the stock of the issuer. When the stock market is rising and, therefore, is expected to continue rising, corporations can borrow by issuing convertibles more cheaply—but at the cost of diluting their stockholders in the future—than they can by issuing bonds. When the stock market falls out of bed, convertibles hit the floor first.

By the same token, easing of money and a recovery of speculative animal spirits invariably see a rise in convertible debenture prices pacing the parallel rise in stock prices. But the professional convertible debenture buyer —and this is a game reserved for professionals—is invariably a borrower, not on margin at the broker's but at the bank, and generally on the basis of 70–80 percent of cost. The professional players of the convertible debenture market accept the risks implicit in such high rates of borrowing. For they expect to make gains plays of 50 percent or better on moves of merely 10 to 15 percent in the stock prices underlying the convertible debenture market. In a rising stock market, the convertible debenture player invariably does.

Traditionally, the bond investor is the investor for income. But the bond market also serves as the speculator's market par excellence. Unlike the stock market, it is a happy hunting ground for the professional speculators who operate on a big scale and on a small margin of their own money.

Timing is the key to successful bond market speculation—specifically, the timing of drops in interest rates. Bond prices jump when interest rates drop. When big-time speculators make money on changes in bond market direction, they make more money than anyone ever makes in stocks. Reason: when banks are looking for loans, bonds are easier to borrow against than stocks. With a 5 percent margin, only $50,000 in cash will buy a speculator (who is big enough to have bank credit) $1 million in government bonds; the other $950,000 is put up by the bank as a loan. The professional speculator can double his money with only a 5-point rise in market price.

The average amateur money-user holds the key to the future—immediate as well as longer term—of America's financial markets. Fortunately for the country and its chances of overcoming the pressures of the financial crisis confronting it, the average investor has been willing to buy bonds for income. So long as good bond yields were above 8 percent, the investor had good reason to feel well rewarded for taking the risk of bailing out the country's best-rated political and financial borrowers. Once yields fell below 8 percent, however, the drop promised a relaxation of borrowing pressures originating with top-rated borrowers.

Normally, the higher top-rated borrowing requirements are admitted to be, the higher the interest rates are expected to be. But the temporary drop in interest rates promised a corresponding drop in inflationary pressures. This has not materialized. The representative cross-section of savers, investors, and ex-speculators who have been buying bonds has been suspicious of any drop in interest rates. And it has been waiting for them to rise again. Eight percent is the dividing line between what the amateur investing public will accept and what the professional dealers in quality paper have found themselves obliged to offer as the alternative to inventorying with their own capital bonds they want to sell and not to hold.

The earnings squeeze of 1971 has been at the root of a corresponding contraction in the tax base throughout America's communities. The result has produced a warning to bond buyers. As corporations have borrowed more and earned less, their bond ratings have suffered an inescapable downgrading. The same process has caught up with the bond issues of state and local governments.

When top- and well-rated corporate bond issues suffer downgrading, the only recourse of the issue in corporations is to sell more stock, diluting their stockholders and adding to the burden of servicing their dividends. When the outstanding bonds of governments suffer a downgrading of market status, their only recourse is to raise more taxes—if the local authorities can win voter approval to do so.

1972 is seeing the crisis of stagflation forcing the most widespread downgrading of bond ratings—corporate as well as tax-free—in recorded history. Bonds able to survive this squeeze will command a credit rating premium in the marketplace. Bonds falling victim to the downgrading process may, and in almost all cases will, continue to pay their interest and remain money-good as to principal. Their yields will rise. The underlying stocks of the corporations whose bonds suffer downgrading will, however, fall to a point where their dividend yields reach record levels.

Meanwhile, the paradox unfolding in the bond market has seen risks there rise while the yields measuring risks have been falling. This is an untenable situation. It augurs an unhappy landing for the tendency of the bond market to be priced upward and to yield less on the assumption that inflation is being cured and stagnation overcome. The stock market will not become safe again until the bond market has.

Q: How will wage-price controls and, possibly, interest rate controls affect the bond market? Do you think bond prices will go lower or will they go up?

Mr. C. C. (Orlando, Florida)

A: The bond market seemingly was helped by the President's emergency program. Its first reaction was to be more encouraged by the half of the program aimed at slowing inflation than to be worried by the other half aimed at speeding up the economy. Its subsequent reaction was to agonize over whether the stubborn slack in the economy would help it more than the equally stubborn push of inflation would hurt it. But the bombshell of runaway government borrowings ended by hurting it more than the promise of inflation control started by helping it.

Q: I am sixty-seven, married with no dependent children. We live within our retirement income plus Social Security. My total assets amount to $135,000 with yields over 6 percent. My objective is safety and income. But to beat the rate of inflation, I feel I need a gross return of 9 percent. I followed your advice last year and bought bonds, but their yield has not been very high. Should I be satisfied with them?

Mr. S. F. (Riverside, California)

A: Reaching for a gross return of 9 percent will expose you to the risk of losses greater than the rate of inflation will. Instead of complaining about the low yield on the bonds you bought last year when I was recommending them to the public, you will do better to crow over the gains you have been accruing on them while interest rates have been falling still lower. Of course, the next rise in interest rates will eat into your paper profits.

Q: I have been a professional stock market investor for thirty years. I have been going to London every October and have found that the lead to trading and investment strategy there paid off if followed here. On my annual checkup there last month, I found to my surprise that, despite the seemingly endless prospect for inflation there, the most sophisticated professional money, with the best performance record, is loading up on the 3 and 4 percent bonds that were issued during the cheap money period. They are selling there at the equivalent of 40 and 50 cents on the dollar—even though many of these bonds will not mature until the mid-1980s.

I have noted in various of your writings your observation that the British experience tends to precede and even to forecast comparable experiences here. Certainly this is true so far as inflation is concerned. Would you recommend adoption of a similar commitment to the so-called deep discount bonds here?

Mr. W. C. J. (New York, N. Y.)

A: Absolutely. In fact, the argument in favor of deep discount bonds is even more persuasive for Americans than for Britishers because so many outstanding American bond issues will mature in the 1970s, bringing the assured capital gain on maturity that much more quickly.

The burden of proof seems to be falling on those with any other preference. Certainly no other investment in bankable capital gains over a reasonable number of years is anything like risk-free. When the people who did well out of stocks during the postwar bull market made their original commitments, they did not expect to turn a fast buck; nor did they. I regard deep discount bonds of medium-term maturity as offering the best of what investors want from both stocks and bonds. Of course, as with all benefits, a corresponding cost is involved—in this case, acceptance of a lower current yield.

Q: How are bond prices quoted? What are "premiums" and "discounts" on bonds?

Mrs. V. N. R. (Denver, Colorado)

A: Bond quotations are based on 100 as equal to par, the face value of the bond. The prices quoted on outstanding bonds are adjusted upward or downward in the bond market as interest rates on new issues fall or rise. The premium in the quoted price of a bond is the percentage amount above par that a purchaser will have to pay for it; conversely, the discount on a bond is the percentage amount below the face value that a purchaser will pay. A bond with a face value of $1,000 quoted at 90 will cost a purchaser $900.

A great many bonds outstanding recently have been quoted at discounts, because of the sustained rise in interest rates over the whole postwar period, a rise that accelerated in the second half of the 1960s. In looking for the yield on discount bonds, remember that the "yield to maturity" takes into account the fact that, whatever the price paid for a bond, the full face value—the par value—is due at maturity. This is why the price rises (and the discount falls) as the date of maturity nears. This appreciation in price, which reaches 100 at maturity no matter how far below current interest rates the nominal rate on the bond is, is taxed as capital gains. Given the low tax rate on capital gains, deep discount bonds with good ratings have become attractive investments to hold as their date of maturity approaches. Deep discount bonds can also be expected to rise in price sharply as and when interest rates head back down to tolerable levels. They and their owners will be the first beneficiaries of a reassertion of control over America's runaway crisis of inflation and under-financing.

One caveat. Extraordinarily deep discounts on bonds reflect the market's professional judgment that there is a more or less serious risk that the issuer will be unable to meet interest payments or to redeem the bonds at maturity. The prices quoted on Penn Central bonds are a case in point. For a really extreme example, there is even a market in Tsarist bonds—which trade for pennies per thousand dollars—on the far-out chance that they may some day be redeemed by the Kremlin! "Super-deep discount" bonds are outright speculations, not investments.

When a bankruptcy actually does happen and the bonds of the bankrupt corporation become totally speculative, until the court works out which of the creditors get what, the trustees issue trustee certificates. These are a sound investment, so sound that they are limited to bank use. Not until after the financial landscape has been strewn with bankruptcies do major capital gains opportunities reappear in "reorganization" bonds. This was a big opportunity during the years of transition between the last bear market and the late bull market.

Q: Which do you recommend, short- or long-term bonds? Would you explain why one is better than the other?

Mrs. J. D. (Tucson, Arizona)

A: Any use of bonds involves a speculation on interest rates and on inflation. Short-term bonds won't yield quite as high a rate of return as long-term bonds, but they will minimize the exposure to still further increases in interest rates, as well as to further inflation. The investor in short-term bonds need not worry about depreciation in market value because of the assurance that repayment will be made in full in a relatively short time.

But investment in long-term bonds that are protected

against call for a substantial number of years is particularly rewarding after a protracted period of rising interest rates because it assures the investor a peak rate of return after yields have begun to fall. The time to go whole-hog in long-term bonds is when interest rates are peaking.

Q: I am sixty years old and hope to work for two more years before retiring. I sold all my stocks this year because the market was making me nervous. I also sold my home and now rent at $335 a month. My entire holdings are $85,000 in savings. My earnings are $7,200. Would investing $80,000 in early maturity, high-quality bonds be a good thing? I would like an 8 percent return on my investment for retirement income.

Mrs. N. N. (Northfield, Illinois)

A: Your idea would be better if early maturity, high-quality bonds had not fallen below 8 percent. A better idea for you any time they are below 8 percent might be "discount" bonds brought out some years ago when interest rates were lower. The trend now is for overborrowings to catch up with underearnings, and for corporate bond ratings to be downgraded.

Depending on their maturity, these bonds are selling at discounts under par ranging up to 40 percent. These discounts reflect their low current return, not the credit ratings of the top-flight companies behind them. As these bonds approach maturity, they will yield built-in capital gains to their holders on top of current returns. Any broker will furnish you with a list.

Q: How much importance should one place on the numerical method of interest protection when evaluating a bond for safety? And what numerical level is excellent, average, poor?

> Mr. C. W. B. (*Austin, Texas*)

A: The higher the number measuring the interest coverage, the safer the bond. The average company with bonds outstanding covers its interest by a margin of 1½ to 2 times. Coverage over 2 times is good to excellent, coverage under 1½ times is poor. The independent credit rating services can be trusted to keep track of bond coverage performance on a current and conservative basis.

Q: *You recently advised a reader to switch her Treasury bonds into corporates or utilities, saying they were of better quality. How can any security be of better quality than one issued by the U. S. government?*

> Mr. J. C. (*St. Petersburg, Florida*)

A: Muscle does not make markets. The bargaining between willing buyers and anxious sellers does. The highest credit ratings are reserved for borrowers who go to the well least often. The fact that the U. S. Treasury and its agencies are borrowing as much and as fast as they can is clouding their credit.

The U.S. government can always use its control over the banking system to force the market to take its paper. Nevertheless, the pricing mechanism of the market is increasingly willing to accept a lower yield on prime corporate debt than on government debt. At the worst of 1970's summer runaway in interest rates on dollar borrowings in Europe, General Motors was paying less for money than Big Uncle.

Now, after the bond market has got free of some of its strains of recent years, bonds of AT&T are offering yields plus built-in gains to maturity approximate to the current yields on federal agency bonds.

Q: I have between $3,000 and $5,000 that I want to invest for income. I was thinking of buying U. S. Treasury notes due in 1977, paying around 8 percent. What is the difference between U.S. Treasury bonds, bills, and notes? And what is the advantage of buying notes?

Mr. C. W. (St. Petersburg, Florida)

A: U.S. Treasury notes bear much shorter maturities than bonds. They fill the gap between Treasury bills and bonds.

The advantage today's Treasury noteholders have over Treasury bondholders is due to present inflationary market conditions. Treasury noteholders can earn the high going rate without being subject to paper losses because of further increases in long-term interest rates, while being assured of getting their money back in the next few years.

Treasury noteholders have another advantage over Treasury billholders due to the recent regulatory change which raised the minimum limit on Treasury bills to $10,000, but let the old $1,000 minimum remain in force on Treasury notes. The government's purpose in raising the minimum limit on bill-buying was to stop the stampede of small savers from lower-yielding passbooks into Treasury bills. Now a new stampede seems to be starting in notes.

So long as Treasury notes remain buyable in $1,000 de-nominations, they seem on the way to becoming as popular with small savers as Treasury bills were before the limit was raised.

Q: In 1970 I bought bonds maturing in 1990 and callable in 1975. Now I find the callable feature means little, as the company can redeem bonds earlier from a sinking fund. In fact, I have just been notified to send half my holdings in for redemption. It also seems I'll only receive par value, although the "callable" feature specifies certain premiums depending on the year called, beginning with 1975. Perhaps you should suggest to your readers that they insist on seeing a sample of the fine print before buying bonds.

Mr. B. L. (Deerfield Beach, Florida)

A: You are absolutely right in your puzzled and shocked assertion that bond buyers take imprudent risks in not checking the fine print in the indentures of even the best grade bonds. Your own painful example leaves you legally defenseless.

The bonds you bought actually provide protection against redemption until April 1, 1975, and then stipulate a premium price of $106.67, which is certainly equitable. The catch is that investors in this $50 million issue are also protected by a sinking fund, which was authorized to begin calling bonds in December of 1971 at par at the rate of $1,300,000 a year. You were one of the unlucky holders whose number came up in this lottery.

Bondholders demanding protection against being hurt in this way have been insisting that sinking fund operations be delayed until after the call protection period has expired. Clearly only top-rated issues can absorb the risk of such a delay.

The moral is that bond investment is every bit as technically intricate as stock or property investment; and that average investors seeking yield and safety protection against today's unprecedented risks do better to rely on the professional managements which run bond funds instead of flying blind.

Q: How and by whom are bonds rated?

Mrs. N. B. (Baton Rouge, Louisiana)

A: By objective and independent rating services, which go by set standards. The ultimate criterion of these standards measures the margin by which bond borrowers can be expected to cover their interest charges and their sinking-fund requirements.

Coverage of fixed charges is taken as a measure of likely ability not to default on interest payments or principal.

Ratings set the rule of the road in credit markets: corporations are sensitive and vigilant in avoiding downgrading in their ratings.

The interest rates bonds bear at issue vary with their ratings. The ratings, starting with the best and going down, are as follows:

Moody's: Aaa, Aa, A, Baa, Ba, B, Caa, Ca, C.

Standard & Poor's:

AAA, AA, A, BBB, BB, B,

CCC-CC, C, DDD-D.

State and local governments, as well as corporations, are subject to this scrutiny and may be downrated while they are outstanding—if the rating services decide that the coverage of interest is more rather than less risky. But the rating services are conservative, and any well-rated government or corporate bond is safe as to interest and principal.

Q: What are AAA bonds, how much do they cost, and where may they be purchased? Plus anything that you think I might need to know about such a bond.

Miss F. M. (Chicago, Illinois)

A: AAA bonds are those enjoying top-quality ratings from the rating services. Bonds issued by the Telephone Company, its regional subsidiaries, and the top blue-chip utilities and industrials qualify. As a practical matter, buyers of AAA bonds overpay for credit insurance: AA-rated bonds and even bonds with lower ratings are just as sure to pay their interest and meet their repayment schedules.

Traditionally, the watershed has separated A's from BBB's, the reason being that fiduciaries are barred from buying BBB's. But 1970's credit squeeze raised the level of the watershed so that the cutoff point above which bonds were deemed to enjoy investment quality fell between the AA's and the A's. The transition is important because if a bond once suffers downgrading from A to BBB, its price is sure to tumble even faster than rising interest rates are forcing bond prices down anyway, and the terms subject to which it can be sold will become more unfavorable.

The way to figure what it costs to buy quality, "money-good" bonds is purely and simply in terms of the yield their interest payments represent. When, for example, the going rate on new AAA issues is set by a 9½ percent coupon, a $1,000 investment will buy $95 of taxable income per annum. If the going rate on new issues rises to 10 percent, $1,000 will buy $100 of annual taxable income. Therefore a bond with a coupon rate of 9½ percent will be worth no more than $950 in the market.

Any bank or broker will buy bonds for you for a small fee.

Q: I am a faithful reader of your syndicated column and admire your market foresight and reasoning. I wonder if you could advise me. I am thirty-five, single, parents deceased. I earn $11,000 as a secretary; have a savings account of $2,000; a $5,000 life insurance policy; and a stock portfolio worth approximately $12,000.

From final settlement of an estate, I now have an additional $5,000 in cash and wish to invest it. Would it be advisable to purchase a corporate bond at the current lower rate of interest? Or should I purchase more stock?

Miss M. O. (Chicago, Illinois)

A: That's quite a dowry you have. And you're entitled to take a hard cold look at any young fellows who express their appreciation of your acumen with the time-honored proposal.

Adding to your earned and unearned income, you might do better buying short-term tax-exempts. Anyway, I recommend not buying quality-rated bonds so long as the market prices them to yield less than 8 percent. And I would not trust any stock to have hit bottom short of its yielding 6 percent against cash earnings at least 40 percent above the dividend payout, while inflation is threatening to continue at a 5 percent rate.

If you marry, you're going to find that you are underinsured. But you're still young enough for the premium to be cheap.

Q: I am over seventy years of age, married and have two married children. I am in the 50 percent income tax bracket. My investments are divided about equally in land, business properties, and stocks. At present I have over $400,000 invested in certificates of deposit and savings. Do you advise replacing my CDs and cash with municipal non-taxable bonds? What is the danger?

Mr. B. R. (Columbus, Ohio)

A: The danger is nil, provided you are willing to accept a lower return for limiting your risk to tax-exempts on bonds issued by communities able to keep their credit ratings. Obviously the ones missing their teachers' payrolls are not.

Q: My wife and I are both thirty-nine, with two young children. We have $2,500 in a teachers' credit union and $1,425 in a mutual fund which has lost value since our investment two years ago. We have no debts and are saving around $250 a month. We are looking for the best way to invest our money. Would municipal bonds be good?

Mr. R. W. (Royal Oak, Michigan)

A: Not for you. Your taxable income as a married teacher with deductions for dependent children is too low to make it worth your while to sacrifice income to earn the lower return paid by tax-exempts. Corporate or government agency bonds will give you a higher yield which you can use.

Q: Are E-bonds still a swindle?

Mrs. R. S. (Spokane, Washington)

A: Definitely. Inflation is quickening the headstart of living costs over present savings returns more cruelly than ever. Whether the E-bond owner knows it or not, the bet on savings bonds is a long-term bet against inflation.

The government has gone to the unusual lengths of admitting that it has been taking advantage of E-bond savers by raising the rate of return. But the swindle is still on because the raised rate in savings bonds is still well below the "money market" rates the Treasury offers the first-class takers of its debt offerings. Also, first-class investors in bonds get their interest currently. Waiting for your return until the end of the road, as savings bond owners have had to do, penalizes the rate of return to allow for the delay in receiving it.

Q: I am retired, aged sixty-two, and I receive a monthly pension of $360, which includes Social Security. Our family is grown and educated and we have no debts; my wife still works. Our home, valued at around $15,000, is paid for. In our investments, we have stressed maximum security and liquidity. We have $10,000 in Series E bonds and $4,000 in certificates of deposit, drawing 5¾ percent interest. I am now thinking of extra income. Would you suggest changing all or a portion of my bonds and certificates into Series H bonds or another type of bond? Or should I leave well enough alone?

Mr. F. B. (Terre Haute, Indiana)

A: I wouldn't buy Series H bonds with Lyndon Johnson's money. You'd do better rolling over in Treasury bills. The minimum is $10,000, and you have it. If you do so during these coming months of rising interest rates, you'll be increasing your income until your wife joins you in retirement. That's the time for the two of you to make a new investment plan.

Q: You have almost convinced me to invest in A-bonds, paying 8 percent. I am recently retired, have several certificates of deposit at 6 percent, due next year, and a few thousand dollars in E-bonds. Would you advise taking my savings money and investing in A-bonds next year?

Mrs. M. D. (Chicago, Illinois)

A: No. To do so would confuse saving with investing. You need to keep your savings reserve intact before you can be in a position to think of investing with responsibility and safety.

You would do better to switch your E-bonds into utility bonds and to keep your savings certificates. Be clear that, at least for the time being, the market yield on government bonds has fallen somewhat below 8 percent.

Q: My husband has been seriously ill and will have to retire soon. We have $38,500 in mutual funds; $4,000 in savings; and no life insurance. We are carrying a mortgage on our $24,000 apartment. We are concerned about our fund investments, as we will need income for the future. What do you suggest?

Mrs. F. E. (Ft. Lauderdale, Florida)

A: I regret your letting a salesman peddle mutual funds to you before you had met the number one family planning requirement represented by life insurance. You are, however, belatedly realistic in identifying income as your need from the capital you cannot risk losing.

Mutual funds will not get it for you. They will also expose you to the danger of short-term loss if your husband's condition puts you in need of cashing in your investment at a time of stock market turbulence. A switch to bonds would be your best move.

Q: I am a widow, past retirement but still employed. I have around $30,000 in two mutual funds, about $7,000 in four blue-chip stocks and a savings account of $3,000. What can I accomplish with this modest portfolio in the next three years when I expect to retire?

Mrs. M. D. (Detroit, Michigan)

A: Give first consideration to accomplishing a positive purpose which, in view of your retirement, is avoiding loss. Avoiding loss also fits into the second objective of a prudent policy for you—the pursuit of income. I suggest switching into bonds. You're smart to be working still. The longer you do, the younger you'll stay. See if the management of your mutual funds offers bond funds into which you can switch without charge.

Q: Now that we are retired, my wife and I are considering moving some of our $35,000 bank savings into top-quality industrial preferred stocks or utilities. What are the merits of cumulative preferred stocks? In years of

*reading your newspaper column, I don't recall an answer
to this question.*

Mr. J. P. (Berwyn, Illinois)

A: I have been nearly as candid about the demerits of
preferred stocks as of savings bonds. Preferred stocks
combine the worst of two worlds: sharing the vulnerability of bonds to increasing interest rates, and the vulnerability of stocks to decreasing earning power.

Cumulative preferred stocks are attractive only after a
depression has done its damage. Only then do accumulated arrearages of unpaid dividends, reflected in depressed prices, offer rich but nonrecurrent capital gains
opportunities.

*Q: When Savings and Loan accounts were paying only
3 percent interest, I bought several shares of a 5 percent
preferred utility stock, at $25.00 a share, and forgot about
them. Now the stock is quoted at $17! My broker says the
only way a preferred can return to par is for interest rates
to be lowered, but this seems remote. I am thinking of
taking my losses now as inflation seems here to stay. Do
you agree?*

Miss S. W. (Columbus, Ohio)

A: Absolutely. But where was your broker when you
were suckered into preferred stock? Of course, easy gen-
eralizations about interest rates will not help you with
this problem. Short-term interest rates can fall, and have,
without helping preferred stocks. Only a significant and
substantial drop in long-term bond yields would. But this

does not seem to be in the cards. Hope you have learned your lesson and will never again invest and forget.

Q: What are index-linked bonds?

Mrs. E. J. A. (Irvington-on-Hudson, New York)

A: They are bonds linked to the cost-of-living index. The purpose of these bonds is to give money the same adjustment deal for renting itself out for interest that labor gets for hiring itself out for wages. For some years it has been standard operating practice in America for annual pay increases written into labor contracts to be supplemented as fast as the cost-of-living index rose. The idea has been to guarantee union members their pay increases in constant dollars. The practice of giving bondholders the same guarantee—of earning their interest in constant dollars—originated in Europe.

The most conspicuous illustration of this new trend was provided in June 1970, when the great Netherlands-based, multinational Phillips Lamp Corporation sold $250 million of bonds in the Euromarket on an index-linked basis.

A big switch is involved in the new practice, and it confirms my working premise that the old textbooks have become hopelessly out-of-date and impractical. They teach that money balks at buying bonds in time of inflation for fear of being paid back in depreciated currency. But the new institution of cost-of-living index-linked bonds is designed to insure the bondholder against this risk. Holders of index-linked bonds are invited to oblige their debtors to load the annual rate of inflation onto the going rate of interest at the time of issuance. The effect of this switch is to turn bondholders from victims of inflation—resisting it—into beneficiaries of inflation—going along with it.

A small trick is also built into this new device of the index-linked bond—the official cost-of-living index has been uniformly understating the rate of inflation. This means that buyers of index-linked bonds, although guaranteed the right to keep up with the Joneses, will not be doing as well as the profiteers from inflation—notably the service-labor trades. Despite the probability that the real cost of living will rise faster than statistical judgments ostensibly keeping pace with it, I expect the practice to grow in America as well as in Europe. And despite the likelihood that the cost of living and of doing business will rise faster than index-linked upward adjustments in supplemental interest payments, I have no doubt that new bond issues will continue to break all records over the long term.

Q: In November 1971, I bought nine Texas East Transmissions bonds for $9,540.00. Later my broker asked me to pay an additional $104.40 for "accrued interest." What did he mean?

Mrs. E. B. (Tavares, Florida)

A: He was wrong not to have charged you for it at the time you paid for your bonds. But he was right to bill you. All good bonds are traded subject to the interest that accrues in favor of their owners between payment dates. The accrued interest item you paid gave the seller his interest for every day he held his bonds between his last interest receipt and the day he sold. You will get the same benefit—unless you pick the precise day of interest payment to sell.

Q: Is it a fair summary of your theory about bond investment that buying good bonds when their yields are high—by which I gather you mean above 8 percent—gives the investor a double in the form of a high return plus a profit when interest rates drop?

Mrs. J. W. (Bloomfield Hills, Michigan)

A: You've got it.

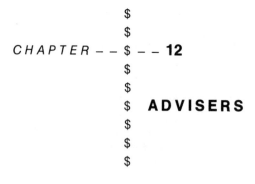

CHAPTER – – $ – – **12**

$ **ADVISERS**

Being negative about advisers is easier than being positive. Ironically, the worse financial advisers do by their clients, the more necessary they continue to become.

Understandably, advisers go with the trend—especially when it seems to point onward and upward. They live in perpetual fear of losing clients because of missed opportunities. Consequently, the riskier conditions become, the more enthusiastic advisers tend to become—although their professional justification is that they will lean into the wind, not run with its currents. Inescapably, the speculative excesses of 1971–72 found the overwhelming majority of financial advisers picking up fees for functioning as cheerleaders instead of as guides.

Mention of financial advisers conjures up images of investment advisers—whether young and "swinging" or sedate and conservative. But the most rudimentary professional advice all money-users need does not begin with investment advice. In this day of big government, tax advisers top the list of money-using counsel.

Auditors and accountants are their professional titles. Jack Seidman, of the prestigious firm of Seidman and

Seidman, is an emeritus member of the austere Accounting Principles Board. In an interview, published with my *Chicago Tribune* column in December 1971, he served notice of the jeopardy implicit in money-users' dependence on advisers. He explained that confidence in the integrity of the figures certified by accountants and auditors provides the indispensable foundation for the job investment advisers take over from their counterparts in the accounting and auditing profession. "In the last depression, it was the bankers who were 'driven out of the Temple'. In the next one," he warned, "the accountants will be the ones to get the boot."

The thrust of his warning was aimed at the blurred standards for reporting earnings. He took as an example the variations condoned in reporting oil industry earnings. Assuming that an oil company has spent a million dollars to drill a successful oil well, there are three ways in which that million dollars can be reflected in the financial statement. One way is to capitalize the million dollars. That way, earnings are not affected at all. A second way is to expense the million dollars and show it as a loss for tax purposes. The third way derives from the second. Accounting for the million dollars as a loss has saved $500,000 in taxes—which then is shown as a reserve to be paid back in the future. Therefore, the same situation can have three possible answers—all acceptable under present rules.

One constructive idea for guarding against costly and sloppy relationships between accounting firms and their clients was put forward by investment adviser John Westergaard in an interview with my *Chicago Tribune* column. He proposed that all corporations be required to change accountants at regular intervals, say every five years, in order to eliminate abuses in the accounting profession. Such a requirement would preclude the development of vested interests and protective devices.

All money-users—including investment advisers as well as managers of corporations and buyers of businesses and business properties—proceed with a built-in dependence on their accounting and auditing advisers. They do in any and every kind of year, but never more so than in the particular year of tax complication 1972 happens to be. The trouble threatening in 1972 and 1973 goes back to a once-in-a-generation combination of planned flexibility for business in its tax accounting of depreciation, and of unbelievable error by the government in preparing its 1970 withholding tax forms. (See Chapters 4 and 6.)

The beginning of wisdom for money-users is to be straight about which specialized advisers—tax, insurance, investment, legal or estate advisers—are worth their keep and for how much.

The cost of legal and accounting services has never been greater or more indispensable. Only the cost of insurance advisory services is constant. The way to deal with insurance salesmen is to begin by finding out how much they stand to make on which kind of policy they have available for sale. And make sure that the cost of whichever form of insurance protection is bought includes the cost of compensation for the salesman—on the fundamental principle that the cost of servicing is marked up into the package paid for.

Great controversy has developed about the appropriate rate of compensation for investment advisers, commonly (but by no means exclusively) known as brokers. For brokers catering to institutional customers, one measure of distress is implicit in the fact that all commissions for trades above $300,000 are negotiable. Thus, professional brokers see less profit in serving professional investors. For amateur investors, the brutal inflation in the cost of hiring responsible money-using investment advice has raised the cost of playing the money-using game. But it is more costly to try to go it alone. Therefore, amateur investors are on notice either to invest less, or to get ready to pay more for services rendered—because trustworthy advisers cannot be expected to work for nothing.

The increasing cost of buying professional advice has helped to make mutual funds attractive for the small investor, since professional money management is part of the deal.

Another way of getting around the problem is to concentrate on conserving money and getting paid in generous drafts of unearned income for the trade-off. Buying good bonds is the best way to do this. It is far better than gambling on fast-talking investment advisers who have no performance record.

Property is another way to conserve money. Although it is virtually impossible to buy a house or land without professional, paid advice, $10,000 will buy you a good deal of property—and buy management and income with it.

Among those who want to stay in the securities market, there are always some who fall back on the opportunistic expedient of trying to get investment advice "on the cheap" from lawyers and accountants. To pay higher legal fees and higher accountants' fees—and get no investment advice—would be a real bargain. For lawyers and accountants notoriously are second only to teachers and preachers as impractical businessmen.

This points out another rule in seeking and accepting investment advice. Ask the person giving it how well he has done in translating his own income into capital. The next question to ask is, "What are you going to make from me?"

If he says he's not going to make anything, watch out! More than incidentally, don't think the advice in my newspaper column is free. The newspapers that buy my columns pay me, and you pay them. You are also paying me by buying this book.

When making arrangements with professional advisers —whether banks, trust companies, mutual funds, insurance firms, investment brokers, accountants, lawyers, or property managers—always be sure that you get straight exactly what the deal is beforehand. Find out what they expect to make, and on what basis, and whether they will make something whether their clients do well or not. Be suspicious if advisers do not ask *you* questions. A good investment adviser should want to know all about your circumstances, your medical expenses, your dependents, your retirement plans, and how much you can afford to lose or to tie up—as well as how long you can sit either with losses or with less than the going rate of return on cash. All advisers want their fees, and are entitled to them. But advisers who do not inquire searchingly into all these factors, and want only their fees, are a one-time shot.

A final word about "do-it-yourself" investment. The number of people capable of managing their own money in the investment markets is small. Possibly it does everybody good to lose some money in an effort to decide what they want to do with it. Choosing professional financial advisers wisely, in turn, depends on the ability to make a clear identification of investment aims. The problem from then on is how to hire enough specialists—for taxes, property, insurance, investment and estate planning —without making the mistake of overhiring or succumbing to the temptation to overpay.

When everything that can be said has been said about advisers, it is important to recognize that any legitimate professional advisers will need to be paid; and to ask bluntly how far ahead of the game you can expect to remain after you have paid them. The answers they give you will provide a valuable basis for evaluating their usefulness to you.

Q: We are approaching retirement age and feel that we need a financial adviser. Our estate of about $200,000 includes earnings, bonds, and common stock. How does one select a financial adviser?

Mr. M. B. (Chicago, Illinois)

A: No question is more difficult. The plight of investors with as much as $250,000, who recognize their dependence on professional advisers but cannot afford the cost, is one of the most serious problems of our economic society. The standard fee is around ¾ of one percent for a minimum of $250,000 under management, or $1,875 a year. You really can't expect it to buy you very much in the way of individual advice. Mutual funds come closest to wholesaling this need of investors too small to buy it for themselves. Ask your broker to suggest six funds with performance records covering years of bad markets and high interest rates. Be sure their stated and demonstrated performance gives top priority to conservation of capital and a high priority to income. Select at least two to switch your common stocks into. Keep a comfortable reserve in savings.

Q: My husband has recently died and I am now faced with managing my affairs. I am anxious to invest money with the aim of getting 7 or 8 percent interest. I am lost and need advice.

Mrs. J. W. (Denver, Colorado)

A: You do need advice—beginning with how to ask for it. There's no prudent way, as you put it, "to invest money." Anyone who might be in a position to help you professionally would first have to know your circumstances: How much have you free for investment over and above cash reserves for emergencies? How much do you need to live on? I suspect that you are one of the many people who cannot afford the cost of even poor advice. Be clear that you're in greater danger of making a false move than of missing any boat.

Q: You have stated if a broker does not do as you wish, change brokers. I have had five and only one really worked for me. But she moved. How do you find a good one?

Mrs. V. H. (Richland, Washington)

A: Your not knowing as a five-time loser suggests that you would do better to quit trying and settle for a couple or three fund managements.

Q: I am an average member of the investing public and I have held back from buying stocks because the commissions are so high. You recently referred to the mass departure of the investing public from the stock market. If commissions were reduced, I believe average investors would return to the market, providing a healthy stimulus. The average investor has been discriminated against by the high commissions.

Mrs. H. R. (Carmel, California)

A: You are right about staying out of the stock market, but for the wrong reason. Because you know so little about it, you are worrying about the cost of commissions instead of the risk of loss. One of the many reasons why the stock market is in trouble is that the brokerage business has been catering to the something-for-nothing psychology you express.

William J. Casey, the extremely capable chairman of the SEC, stated in an interview in my newspaper column that he would have no confidence in any investment adviser not operating at a profit against today's still rising costs of doing business. The stock market would be a safer place for amateurs like you if you were paying higher commissions plus service charges for better investment advice.

Incidentally, most firms charge their salesmen a $15 handling fee on all tickets written. This works out as a protection for the customer because it takes the profit out of "churning."

Q: I intend to make a $5,000 investment soon. Certain well-known companies will manage your funds and make investments for you for $200 a year, and agree to try and

*do their best to make your money make money faster
than you can. What do you think of these companies?*

*A very large and well-known brokerage house also told
me that they believed they could do better than the
above companies at only the cost of the commission on
each transaction each time they buy and sell. What is
your opinion?*

Mr. C. P. (Chicago, Illinois)

A: You will do well to ponder Ben Franklin's remark
that a fool and his money are soon parted.

Costs being what they are, I cannot possibly see how
any advisory firm can afford to handle any account for a
minimum fee of only $200 a year. Most firms of standing
found themselves obliged, before costs rose to anything
near their present level, to put a minimum of many times
$5,000 on the advisory accounts they will accept. I think
they were right. I suspect that you are confusing your
idea of an advisory bargain with the profit motive.

Your money problem is that you have too little to play
with and too little to buy advice with. But you have a
problem that is even more fundamental than your money
problem—you do not know what you are doing. I cannot
believe that a brokerage firm expressed any such confidence as you report. It sounds to me like you are confusing the inappropriate fast talk of a commission-hungry
salesman with a responsible assurance from the firm in
question. The firm would be bound to lose money on any
such deal with you—that is, unless it "churned" your account in order to make commissions as fast as it traded
you out of your remaining money.

Q: What is your opinion of investment managing firms? Where can one check on their performance? One firm claims a 34 percent average return and only accepts accounts of $10,000 and up. We have just $10,000 to invest and wonder whether subscribing to such a service would be wise. We already have $6,000 in a mutual fund and a trust fund of $6,000.

Mrs. R. E. T. (Spokane, Washington)

A: Counselling firms observe a high standard of ethics, but the only public check on their performance is offered by those which operate mutual funds. Check the credentials and client references of any firm offering to accept accounts as small as $10,000 for individual supervision. The bare minimum for most is $100,000. I'd also be very dubious of any claim suggesting that a 34 percent return would be par for the course.

Mutual funds literally mutualize investment advice for people unable to afford to hire their own. I think your best bet is to put the $10,000 into a fund. Check on your present fund's performance before deciding whether to add to it or diversify.

Q: I am a widow, age sixty-nine. I will have about $500,000 to invest in about four months. I am thinking about putting this in United States Treasury bonds. What do you think? Should they be long-term?

Mrs. E. F. G. (Cincinnati, Ohio)

A: You could not possibly do worse. You need an investment adviser, and you can afford to pay for a good one. Ask at least three to recommend a program designed primarily to conserve your capital; and, secondarily, to take minimal risk for a moderate rate of return.

Q: I have a trust agreement with my bank to manage $100,000 worth of stock I recently inherited. They charge one-half of one percent for this service which, since I know nothing about the stock market, seems like a bargain to me. Do you agree?

Mr. R. F. G. (Butte, Montana)

A: By your own account, you need a shepherd. Your bank is charging you the standard, going, professional rate for investment advice. Ask not how much your trust adviser is charging you, but how prudent and profitable his advice is. Ask also whether an institution can pay a competent staff after billing you a mere $500 a year and still make out. Your apparent bargain may be its disaster and yours.

Q: In 1969, I sold my blue-chip holdings and invested in long-term industrial bonds. On the advice of my broker, I also bought $10,000 in Canadian oil bonds. I later found that Canada deducts 15 percent from my interest check as their income tax. I was not informed that this was a Canadian issue, and it reduces the income I need. What is my recourse to recover this annual loss?

Mr. N. W. (Chicago, Illinois)

A: Get a different broker. If it's any consolation to you, the 15 percent withholding collected by Canada is a deduction from your United States income tax.

Q: A few minutes after noon one day, my broker told me he did not have a buyer for the 200 shares of stock I had ordered sold earlier. Between that time and exchange closing, the stock went up by $3.00, but I received the lowest price. Can I find out the time the stock went up?

Mrs. D. J. D. (Chicago, Illinois)

A: Either your broker—whom I hope you are in the process of firing—didn't give you the straight story or you didn't get it straight. Nevertheless, the way the market works is not as the result of brokers with sell orders looking for buyers. Your particular stock is listed on the New York Stock Exchange. The New York Stock Exchange keeps track of the time of each transaction in its listed securities. Check your records and your recollection and write to their complaint department. They can give you a complete rundown.

Q: My problem is not what stocks or bonds to buy, but how to get delivery of what I do buy. I order bonds which don't arrive after six weeks elapse.

The broker says he is unable to do anything to expedite delivery. The Stock Exchange rules state that payment must be made in five days and delivery made in thirty days. Apparently they can still enforce payment but they look out the window on delivery dates. Is there anything that can be done? If the brokerage firm goes broke in the meantime, will I have to take what they give me for my bonds after liquidation?

Mr. B. K. (Boca Raton, Florida)

A: Answering your first question, write the Stock Exchange and hope for the best. But start shopping for a better broker. The new government-sponsored Securities Investor Protection Corporation provides the answer to your second question.

If you are foolish enough not to have your securities transferred out of your broker's name and your firm goes bad, you will now receive back all fully paid securities which are identifiable.

But if your securities are not identifiable, or if there is an uncompleted transaction, you will receive up to a total of $50,000—$30,000 in securities and $20,000 in cash.

SIPC is designed to help the small amateur stockholder. The professionals know enough to avoid the risk.

Q: Is $160 a year too much to pay for a weekly newsletter on the business situation?

Mr. N. P. (Cedar Rapids, Iowa)

A: If you get one good money-saving or money-making idea out of your subscription, it's a bargain.

Q: How can I find out whether American Micro Devices and Western Standard Uranium are registered in Illinois? Do I consult a broker?

Miss R. R. (Chicago, Illinois)

A: You might enjoy more peace of mind not knowing. Anyone amateurish enough to feel impelled to ask such questions is better off not reaching beyond the mainstream of money use.

Q: Whenever I've invested in real estate or stocks, I've given them the kiss of death. At the moment I own 2,000 shares of a $3.50 stock which I bought at $4.25 on a tip from one of my successful friends. It was supposed to hit 13 in six weeks. This has been my first and last "tip." I'm selling out.

Mr. A. S. (*Highland Park, Illinois*)

A: You strike me as having earned your "R" for realist. Your luck won't change so long as you go on taking tips on junk. Perhaps your "friend" is successful because he gives tips like this one instead of acting on them for himself.

Q: Three years ago, I purchased $25,000 worth of rare coins. A lawyer friend of mine told me that rare coins are a good investment to beat inflation. Even though the stock market has shown a good recovery, rare coins are dirt cheap. What would my best move be at this time?

Mr. O. L. (*Chicago, Illinois*)

A: Beware of lawyers giving investment advice. Collectors' items and genuine treasures do enjoy scarcity value appreciation whether inflation is a problem or not. For example, old English silver has been a highly profitable investment though silver itself has not been working out well as a speculation.

Your experience is nearly as bad as if you had been waiting for the price of gold to double during the years of high interest rates before it did, when gold paid nothing and bonds paid enough to double your money without speculating. Unless you know what you are doing in a professionally sophisticated way—and I doubt that you do —I think that you would be better off resisting the lure of this siren song. I suggest that you take the trophies you have been stuck with to a collector and try to get out even.

Q: In order to avoid taxes on the $135,000 sale of a piece of property, we have been advised to put the money in a living trust.

Mr. F. W. (Palatine, Illinois)

A: I'm afraid you have been ill-advised. If you have made a gain on the property, you will owe tax whether you put the money in a trust or not. Consult an accountant—investment questions often boil down to tax questions. A broker is no help in this kind of situation.

INDEX

$
$
$
$
$
$
$
$
$

273